C000319871

# SEVILLE & ANDALUCÍA

BY
JOHN GILL

Produced by
Thomas Cook Publishing

**Written by** John Gill

**Original photography by** Michelle Chaplow
**Original design by** Laburnum Technologies
Pvt Ltd

Editing and page layout by Cambridge
Publishing Management Limited,
149B Histon Road, Cambridge CB4 3JD

Published by Thomas Cook Publishing
A division of Thomas Cook UK Ltd

PO Box 227, The Thomas Cook Business Park, Units 19–21,
Coningsby Road, Peterborough PE3 8XX, United Kingdom
E-mail: books@thomascook.com
www.thomascookpublishing.com

ISBN: 1-841571-90-3

Text © 2003 Thomas Cook Publishing
Maps © 2003 Thomas Cook Publishing
First edition © 2003 Thomas Cook Publishing

Head of Publishing: Donald Greig
Project Editor: Charlotte Christensen
Project Administration: Michelle Warrington
DTP: Steven Collins

Printed and bound in Spain by: Grafo Industrias Gráficas, Basauri

Cover: Plaza España, Seville. Photograph by J. Arnold/jonarnold.com
Inside cover: Photographs supplied by Spectrum Colour Library

CD manufacturing services provided by business interactive ltd, Rutland, UK.
CD edited and designed by Laburnum Technologies Pvt Ltd

# Contents

# Introduction

From the conquistadores to Carmen, and from the Reconquest to the *corrida* or bullfight, Seville has for centuries been seen as the quintessential Spanish city. Both Columbus and Magellan set sail for the Americas from here. It is the home of flamenco and the *cante jondo* ('deep song'), the raw vocal form at the centre of flamenco. The vast tobacco factory at its centre where Prosper Mérimée set his tragic love story of Carmen and Don Juan is now one of Spain's largest universities.

The city's celebrations for the Easter *Semana Santa*, or holy week, are the most exuberant in Spain. Twice during the 20th century the city was chosen to showcase Spain in two World Expositions: the 1929 Ibero–American Exposition and the 1992 Expo. And for anyone lucky enough to live in or near

Seville's La Giralda

the Andalucían capital, of the region's three great cities – Seville, Granada and Córdoba – it is the most vibrant, most cultured and most resistant to the tourism that threatens to swamp parts of Granada and Córdoba.

There has been a human settlement on the site of Seville ever since the Greeks and Phoenicians began exploring the western Mediterranean (the latter founded Cádiz, said to be the oldest town in Europe, in 1100 BC). By AD 47 it was an important Roman military and trading base, as can be seen at Roman sites such as Italica (founded in 206 BC) just north of Seville and at other sites elsewhere in Andalucía.

Despite being isolated at the southwesternmost tip of Europe, neither Seville nor Andalucía as a whole evaded the Visigoth invasions of the 4th century AD. Converted to Christianity, the northern invaders turned Seville into a centre for learning, trade and culture.

The Visigoths were themselves supplanted in AD 711 by the arrival of the region's most advanced civilisation, the north African Moors, who spread swiftly through the region and left an indelible impression on its cities, landscape and culture. Water technologies introduced by the Moors transformed the near-desert landscape of most of the region, and the new rulers appear to have been comparatively liberal, allowing both Christians and Jews to practise their trades and religions.

As the Moorish influence fanned out across the Iberian peninsula, stretching beyond what is now Barcelona on the Mediterranean coast and almost as far as the modern Portuguese border on the Atlantic coast, the region's disparate Catholic kingdoms, forced north by the Moorish invasion, began to take their lands back. The 'Reconquest' of Spain,

launched in the 11th century, pushed the Moors back south, until the last Moorish king, Boabdil, was forced to leave Granada in 1492.

With the *reyes catolicos*, the Catholic kings, in the ascendant, Seville was ideally positioned for the golden age of Spanish expansionism. By the beginning of the 16th century it was the centre of all trade with the new territories in the Americas. For two centuries, until the rio Guadalquivir (Guadalquivir river) began to silt up and trade shifted to Cádiz, Seville was in effect the centre of the Spanish universe. Although power and trade had moved on by the 18th and 19th centuries, Seville remained, and still remains, Andalucía's most sophisticated city. After Madrid and Barcelona, it is the most sophisticated in Spain.

Quayside houses in Triana, Seville

# The City

Even though it is nearly three times larger than its sibling, Granada, Seville is a remarkably compact city. The city centre consists of four key *barrios*, or districts: Santa Cruz, La Macarena, El Arenal and Parque de María Luisa. Most of the key sights are within walking distance of each other: the Giralda tower and cathedral and Reales Alcázares palaces and gardens in Santa Cruz; the Plaza de España and the pavilions of the 1929 Exposition.

Seville's Plaza de España

## Lifestyle

The enduring appeal of Seville lies as much in the lifestyle led by its people on its streets as in the grandeur of the historic monuments that loom above them. The mythology insists that, among all the Spanish peoples, the Andalucíans are the wildest, the most passionate, and the most likely to throw a party or hold a parade at the drop of a hat.

The Sevillanos, the mythology continues, are even worse, as can be observed at the annual *Semana Santa* (holy week), leading up to Easter Sunday, when *nazarenos* (penitents) in the pointed hoods and robes of the Inquisition march through the neighbourhoods day and night in a celebration that culminates in an all-night street party. After a short breather of a week or so, the Sevillanos then plunge back into the madness of the *Feria de Abril*, the April Fair, which is the largest in Spain. As the visitor soon discovers, barely a month, or fortnight, passes in Andalucía without some excuse for a party.

## A Working City

Seville is also different from any of the other Andalucían cities in remaining its own city. While some of its historic buildings may be on the world monument circuit, Seville is still a city catering to the needs and whims of its inhabitants. It is a working city, with a large student culture based around its central university which supports a wide variety of concerts and music festivals, cinemas and theatres, bookstores and record shops, nightclubs and, of course, a wide spectrum of healthily stroppy student activism.

## Street Culture

It is also a city where you will find yourself thrown into the culture as soon as you step outside: unless you hide in your hotel, you will find yourself having breakfast, lunch and dinner elbow-to-elbow with the Sevillanos. Indeed, despite those periods when Atlantic weather systems push up the Guadalquivir valley to drench Seville, much of life is conducted out of doors, even in winter, when the bars of Santa

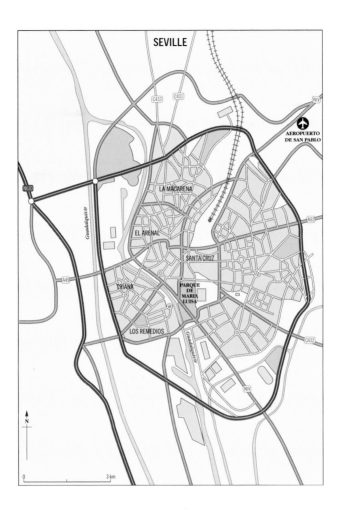

Cruz, Triana and Macarena deploy pavement heaters to warm their patrons. In the outdoor bars around calles Mateos Gago and Rodrigo Caro in Santa Cruz, it is possible to plunge into the street culture of Seville in the shadow of its two greatest cultural monuments: La Giralda tower and the façades of both the cathedral and the Reales Alcázares.

## Exploring Andalucía

Seville is also a near-perfect centre for wider exploration: by train, bus or car to Jerez and Cádiz, or north to Huelva, east to Córdoba, Granada or Málaga. If, that is, you can drag yourself away.

# Landscape and People

Seville's outlying provinces – Huelva, Cádiz, Málaga, Jaén, Granada and Almería – represent almost every type of terrain you might encounter in Spain. From marshland to the highest mountain on mainland Spain; from rolling temperate farmland, sandy orange groves and olive plantations to bleak lunar desert and fantastical dune systems; and from the congested beaches of the Mediterranean to the wild and empty strands of the Atlantic Costa de la Luz – Andalucía seems to contain the whole of Spain in miniature.

Zahara de los Atunes in Cádiz province

### A Man-made Landscape

It is in fact largely a man-made landscape, which we can date back to AD 711, when Tariq ibn Ziyad, governor of Tangier, came ashore at the region's southernmost point with an army of 10,000 Berbers, intent on expanding his dominion into Europe.

As well as their architecture and sciences, the Muslim north African Berbers brought with them the water technologies that had helped them transform desert oases into arable farmland. Sea trade brought citrus fruits, cereals and ground crops, just as earlier traders had brought the hardy olive and fig from the Fertile Crescent.

Seville's history is inextricably linked to its trade, both domestic and overseas, and how it has managed its surrounding landscape. The Moors brought the sandy valleys and plains to life, and wealth flowed through the region's cities. The end of the bitter Reconquest ushered in a period of *latifundismo* (absentee

landlordism) in which vast tracts of land were awarded to regional dukes and generals as a reward for supporting the Catholic monarchy's fight against the Moors. The effects of *latifundismo* can still be seen today in those beautiful, endless vistas of farmland with the odd crumbling farm building in the distance. The *latifundistas* (landlords) frequently controlled their lands at a distance from Seville and other cities, leaving *caciques* (foremen) to run a brutal regime over disenfranchised day labourers. Hundreds of thousands left the land for the slums of the big cities, and as late as the 19th century forced emigration was bringing large numbers from regions such as northerly Asturias to work the land. *Latifundismo* unwittingly also tilled the soil for a rich harvest of anarchist uprisings across Andalucía and elsewhere in the 18th and 19th centuries, provoking state counter-violence and, ultimately, the dissatisfactions that led to the Civil War.

## The People

Seville and its outlying regions might, given its history over the past two or three thousand years, lay claim to the title of the most ethnically diverse region of Europe. While much of Europe was overrun by sundry Vandal and Goth invasions, Seville sat at the centre of an intense cultural and ethnic trade between northern Europe, the eastern Mediterranean, Africa, the Caribbean and Central and South America that continues in part today. From the Moorish features that peer out from the faces of people in the remote *pueblos blancos* to the *n*th generation Hispano–Americans and Hispano–Africans in the cities and ports, Andalucía has spent millennia as a cultural melting pot at a point where three continents meet. It is not without its problems, but compared to the rest of Europe it remains a markedly diverse and tolerant place.

Girasols – sunflowers – are one of Andalucía's most ubiquitous crops

# History

| | |
|---|---|
| **30,000 BC(?)** | Estimated age of palaeolithic cave drawings found in La Cueva de Pileta, Montejaque, Serrania de Ronda mountains. |
| **15,000–7000 BC** | Spread of farming and settlements begins to overtake hunter-gatherer cultures, spreading from the Fertile Crescent (modern-day Middle East) westwards. |
| **4000 BC** | Burial mound in Granada province from this date contained clothing, including shoes, religious offerings and other gifts. At roughly the same time, animal husbandry or cattle breeding begins. |
| **2200 BC** | Bronze Age artefacts from this period found in dolmen burial chambers at Millares, Almeria. |
| **1100 BC** | Founding of Cádiz, said to be Europe's first city, by Phoenician adventurers on lagoon at mouth of rio Guadalete (Guadalete river). |
| **600 BC** | Greek traders arrive on Mediterranean coast, likely importers of earliest olive trees. |
| **500 BC** | Carthage colonises southern part of peninsula. |
| **206 BC** | Romans defeat Carthaginians, begin construction of Italica (5km/3.1 miles north of modern Seville). |
| **AD 415** | Visigoths from northern Europe's modern-day Baltic regions invade Spain. |
| **446** | Spain under Visigoth control. |
| **590** | First Visigoth conversions to Catholicism. |
| **711** | Tariq ibn Zayid, governor of Tangier, lands a 10,000-strong Berber army near Tarifa. |
| **756** | Independent Moorish emirate declared in Cordoba. |
| **1085** | First decisive victory of Catholic Reconquest at Toledo. |
| **1147** | Almohads take Seville and regions, begin construction of Torre del Oro and Giralda tower. |
| **1236** | Christians retake Córdoba. |

| | | | |
|---|---|---|---|
| **1248** | Christians retake Seville. | **1630** | Madrid overtakes Seville as the largest city in Spain. |
| **1469** | Marriage of Fernando of Aragon and Isabel of Castilla unites the kingdoms of Castilla and Aragon. Fernando and Isabel prosecute the Reconquest with vigour. | **1701–13** | War of the Spanish Succession in which the Habsburg kings are supplanted by the Bourbon dynasty. |
| **1480** | Inquisition established in Seville. Among its first victims are homosexuals, Jews and, later, protestants and Mudéjars (Moors who were 'allowed to stay'). | **1713** | Under the Treaty of Utrecht, Britain takes control of Gibraltar. |
| | | **1717** | With the rio Guadalquivir silted and no longer navigable, trade with the Americas moves to Cádiz. |
| **1492** | The last Moorish redoubt, Granada, falls to the Christians. Columbus sails for the Americas funded by the Spanish throne. | **1804–14** | Peninsula War in which Britain sides with Spain against French control of parts of Spain. |
| **1519** | Hernán Cortés conquers Peru. | **1805** | Battle of Trafalgar off Cabo Trafalgar (Cape Trafalgar), north of Tarifa, between Britain and Spain. |
| **1532** | Ferdinand Magellan embarks on the first circumnavigation of the world. | | |
| **1580** | Seville is officially declared the largest city in Spain. | **1811–12** | Spanish radicals establish the Cortes, or Spanish Parliament, in Cádiz, under a state of siege. The liberals are defeated by Bourbon king Fernando VII but set a template for a future constitution. |
| **1588** | Spanish Armada launches and loses an attack on the British fleet in the English Channel. | | |
| **1609** | King Felipe III orders expulsion of all Moors from Spain. | **1833** | Disputes between conservative Fernando VII and liberal Carlos IV |

| | |
|---|---|
| | lead to the First Carlist War. |
| 1846 | Second Carlist War. |
| 1872 | Third (and final) Carlist War. |
| 1873 | Shortlived First Republic established, but founders due to inability to control Spain's regions. Monarchy restored in 1874. |
| 1881 | Pablo Picasso born in Málaga. |
| 1882 | Worsening conditions for farm workers in western Andalucía, in particular around Seville, lead to increasing unrest. |
| 1895–8 | Spain loses Cuba during the US-backed Cuban War. |
| 1910 | La Confederación Nacional del Trabajo (National Labour Confederation, or CNT) founded in Seville by embryonic anarchists following Russian theorists such as Mikhail Bakunin. |
| 1917 | Start of three years of anarchist uprising across Andalucía. |
| 1923 | General Miguel Primo de Rivera stages military coup, winning support with promises to modernise state and economy. |
| 1929 | The great Ibero–American Exposition coincides with the Wall Street Crash (30 November). |
| 1930 | Effects of the Depression unseat Rivera, who is replaced in 1931 by a new Second Republic, one riven by factional dispute. |
| 1936 | Tensions between the right-wing Falange and the disorganised left-wing Popular Front break out into open Civil War. Among the Falange's leaders is Francisco Franco, who is made head of state. |
| 1939 | The Civil War ends with defeat for the left. Franco keeps Spain out of the Second World War, but Spain is boycotted by the United Nations, forcing the nation, Andalucía particularly, into *los años de hambre* (Years of Hunger), during which many starve. |

| | |
|---|---|
| **1975** | Franco's death brings about the end to his absolute dictatorship. Franco favourite Bourbon Juan Carlos becomes King Juan Carlos I and seizes moment to modernise Spain's democracy and economy. |
| **1982** | El Partido Socialista Obrero Español (Spanish Socialist Workers' Party, PSOE) is voted into power. |
| **1982** | Andalucía becomes an autonomous region governed from Seville. |
| **1985** | Border with Gibraltar opened after 25-year blockade. |
| **1986** | Spain joins the EU. |
| **1992** | Expo 92 puts Seville and Spain back on the world stage. |
| **1996** | After 14 years of PSOE government, Spain elects the centre-right Partido Popular (PP), led by former tax inspector José María Aznar. |

# Moorish Spain

While it is tempting to consider Seville's 'Golden Age', when it was at the forefront of Spain's conquest of the Americas, as its defining historic achievement, the Moorish invasion of Spain nearly a millennium earlier left a far more lasting impression on the city, its surrounds and what would become the modern nation.

At the height of its expansion in the 16th century, Spain's dominion spread as far south as the Cape Verde Islands off Senegal, and west to Cuba, other parts of the Caribbean, and a large swathe of the American mainland from southern California down to Peru. Briefly, at the turn of the 18th century, it even controlled part of what is now Holland.

As we can see today from the Andalucían countryside, the Moors laid an agricultural foundation without which much of the region would have remained scrubby desert. Without agriculture, neither the Moors nor their Christian successors could have fed, clothed or financed the villages and towns that in turn supported Seville and other cities.

Of course, the Moors' chief contribution to Spain was intellectual. Over the several centuries and eras of Moorish rule, they introduced medicine, mathematics, languages, philosophy and law, among other disciplines. In the 12th century Córdoba alone produced the philosopher and physician Averroës (1126–88) and the Jewish philosopher, jurist and physician, rabbi Moses ben Maimon, more commonly known as Maimonides (1135–1204), the 'father' of modern medicine.

The Moors' most notable contribution was architectural, although few contemporary citizens would have had access to these ornate marvels. As well as the great palaces at Seville, Granada and Córdoba, they built lesser but no less exquisite monuments at Medina Azahara, Ronda, and the *alcazabas* (fortresses) at Almería and Málaga.

As well as slipping unobtrusively into the Andalucían and Spanish gene pool, the Moors had a profound effect on Spain and its neighbours to the north. Just as Averroës translated Aristotle and introduced his thinking to western Europe, so other Moorish thinkers and teachers built a bridge between the eastern Mediterranean and western Europe, at a time when western Europe was still mired in the Dark Ages.

Centuries of history written by northern European historians have interpreted the 'Reconquest' as an honourable campaign to rid Spain of barbarians, although today it might be seen more as ethnic cleansing. (On the subject of cleansing, it might also be added that the Moors, with their elaborate *hammams* or baths, showed unwashed Europe where the soap was.) Yet it seems that the Moors lived alongside Christians and Jews as amicably as any medieval cultures might, and practised a tolerance notably absent in the attitudes of the Christian victors of the Reconquest. Certainly, Ferdinand and Isabel gave the Inquisition free rein to persecute anyone – first the Moors, then Protestants and Jews, then Moors who had converted to Christianity – whose beliefs and practices were at odds with Catholicism. The forces of the Reconquest, a monarchy and elite aristocracy backed by the armed forces, would spend the subsequent three or so centuries vigorously resisting any emancipation of citizenry, land, law or state.

The *conquistadores* may have garlanded the cathedrals and palaces of Seville and its neighbours with fantastic jewels and gold plundered from the New World, but it is likely that without the foundation of civilisation laid by the Moors, their boats might not even have reached Sanlúcar de Barrameda.

Above: The façade of the Alcazar in Seville
Left: Moorish architecture – Córdoba's magnificent Mezquita

# Governance

Any European country where as recently as 1981 factions in the military thought they could incite a coup by holding its parliament hostage has to have an interesting political history.

Andalucía's parliament

The coup attempt of 23 February 1981 led by Colonel Antonio Tejero Molina was both a test and a proof of Spain's brand new (1977) democracy. Tejero and his men held the Cortes, or parliament, hostage for 24 hours before surrendering. Interestingly, the man responsible for the coup's failure was King Juan Carlos I, who had used Franco's death as an excuse to usher in a new, modernising democracy. Tejero's rebels, controlled by shadowy figures higher up the armed forces hierarchy, claimed that Carlos supported the coup. When the king informed the country's top generals that he opposed the coup, it fell apart.

The green and white Andalucían flag

While disturbing at the time, the attempted coup proved to most Spanish people that their young democracy was robust enough to withstand armed insurrection.

For centuries, a grotesque imbalance of wealth and power undermined any attempts to stabilise Spanish politics. The advent of *latifundismo,* the distribution of great tracts of land to cronies after the Reconquest, only intensified the disparity, especially in Andalucía, which was the largest and most agricultural of all Spain's regions.

Even the 'Golden Age' of global conquest and trade did little more than enrich the already wealthy, and perhaps ease the appearance of a new, educated middle class. It took revolution and the industrialisation of northern Europe to suggest different models of politics.

Spain was not alone in watching the French Revolution (1789–99) with interest. Greece, for example, began to plot the overthrow of the Ottoman Empire. Spanish radicals had attempted to establish a liberal constitution in Cádiz in 1812, only for it to be quashed by Fernando VII. It was the knock-on effect of industrialisation in northern Europe – negligible in Andalucía, but Barcelona's cotton trade rivalled Manchester's in the mid-19th century –

Ronda's monument to Blas Infante, founder of the Andalucísmo independence movement

that set in motion the forces that would transform Spain.

Social unrest began to spread across southern Spain in the mid-19th century, despite failed attempts at republican government. In 1923 General Primo de Rivera launched a military coup that would rule until 1930. In 1931 the Second Republic was established, prompting the far right to launch the Falange two years later. Increasing tensions between the two sides broke out into Civil War, with General Franco becoming head of state in 1936. Spain remained under his dictatorship until his death in 1975.

Innovations in government were frozen during the Franco years, while behind the scenes a Kafkaesque bureaucracy flourished. Only in 1976, when King Juan Carlos I appointed Adolfo Suárez prime minister, did Spain begin to see a semblance of parliamentary democracy. In 1982, open elections brought the Partido Socialista Obrero Español (PSOE), the Spanish Socialist Workers' Party, to power. Fourteen years later José María Aznar led the centre-right Partido Popular (PP), the People's Party, to victory, and won again in 2000.

Less than 30 years of parliamentary freedom have seen Spain accelerate into line with the rest of Europe and the EU. It continues to devolve power to its 14 autonomous regions, and within those to the independent provinces, such as, in Andalucía, Cádiz, Málaga and Jaén.

# Culture

The spiritual home of flamenco, Seville and its neighbouring regions share a culture that not only stretches back thousands of years to pre-Christian festivals, but also looks forward with a lively avant-garde that can rival Barcelona and Madrid.

Dancing a *sevillana*

## The Cultural Influence of Andalucía

This culture has produced or been adopted by numerous painters – not least Velazquez, Picasso, Zurbarán, Goya, Murillo and Bomberg – and writers – famously, poets Federico Garcia Lorca, Luis Cernuda and Antonio Machado, and earlier figures such as Lope de Vega and peripatetic legend Cervantes. It has also been adopted by contemporary figures such as novelist Juan Goytisolo, and needless to say has attracted a lengthy queue of others ready to pledge their *afición* (fondness) for city and region, not least Rilke, Joyce, Borges, Hemingway, Laurie Lee and Orson Welles.

Carnaval balladeers

## Music and Dance

As well as producing Cádiz's favourite musical son, Manuel de Falla, Seville and its regions also gave the world no less than two legends of classical and flamenco guitar, Andres Segovia and Paco de Lucia, not to mention dancer Cristina Hoyos.

The thriving university cities, most notably Seville itself, Granada and Cádiz, have generated an energetic youth culture, particularly since *la movida*, 'the movement', swept away the restrictions of the Franco era in the early 1980s. A noisy underground has produced post-punk and electro bands such as Largartija Nick and Los Planetas, and perhaps uniquely across Europe, Andalucían nightclubs and concerts segue between contemporary dance culture and traditional flamenco and other indigenous folk and popular styles, with audiences displaying equal enthusiasm for both. (It is also interesting to note that there is no upper age 'limit' on entry to these events.)

Perhaps because Andalucía sits at a junction between three continents, north African, eastern Mediterranean and Central/South American influences are often as recognisable as those from northern Europe or the United States in

Spanish popular music. This mixture might best be heard in the work of cult 'world' music band Radio Tarifa. And again perhaps uniquely in European popular music, this is popular music sung in the band's own language.

The home of flamenco (*see p20*) has long had an aversion to the north American invention, jazz, but in recent decades it has produced world-class jazz musicians such as Tete Montoliu. Of a newer generation, Seville's Chano Domingo is just one Andalucían who has translated to the world circuit, and contemporary flamenco giant Enrique Morente (*see p21*) makes frequent sorties into the world of jazz. Seville, Granada and Cádiz all have annual festivals that span many of the arts, and some hold specialist jazz or ethnic music festivals.

Seville's world-class Maestranza opera house

## A Passion for Culture

Much of Spain's cultural life was stifled or went underground during the Franco era and given that it has had less than a quarter century since *la movida* to catch up with the 'outside' world, it has pursued it with a voracious appetite. Andalucíans, and the Spanish in general, are passionate about culture like no other European country, and have an open-mindedness that could offer a lesson to the rest of the world.

Hooded *nazarenos* at Easter

# Flamenco

Flamenco, the archetypal Andalucían musical form that for many *is* the sound of Spain, has long been in dire need of demystifying, nowhere more so than the matter of those castanets. These should be followed swiftly by the gaudy polka-dot gypsy dresses that Spanish women wear to dance the *sevillana*, in turn often mistaken as the 'authentic' flamenco dance.

All three of the above 'customs' are almost wholly alien phenomena grafted on to flamenco in the 20th century, much to the anguish of some of flamenco's more traditionalist performers and *aficionados*.

Few histories of flamenco will agree on its origin. Many will concur that it took root among the East European Roma, or gypsy, population who arrived in Spain in the 18th century. Some go back further, to the 15th century and the transition of Arabic folk from the lute to the guitar. Others point to the fascinating recurrence of song forms, themes and instrumentation among folk musics around the Mediterranean littoral. Some even track flamenco back to Roman times.

What all historians agree on, however, is how difficult it can be to hear the real thing today. Flamenco's seed-bed, the cafés, bars and clubs of 19th-century Seville and Granada, gave way to a commercialised entertainment, the *tablao* (show, or tableau), at the turn of the 20th century. Even the once notorious flamenco caves of the gypsy Sacromonte area of Granada became tourist attractions, with the result that the *gitanos* tended to keep their (usually ad hoc) celebrations to themselves and their friends. It requires a certain detective work, or at least reliable contacts, to locate bona fide flamenco today.

The fundament of flamenco is the vocal form known as *cante jondo* ('deep song'), originally and often today unaccompanied, apart from hand percussion. It is here that we locate the essence of flamenco, *duende* ('imp' or 'goblin' in English, but meaning 'spirit').

Like swing, or the blues, *duende* is an unquantifiable spirituality glimpsed fleetingly during a performance of great passion. It is most commonly found at gitano *juergas*, private parties, and is as likely to be produced by the joint effects of liquor and cocaine as the muse. The greatest *cantaor* (male singer) of the 20th century, El Camarón, died from excesses of drink and drugs aged 40 in 1992.

*Danzas* or *bailes* (both meaning 'dances') soon began to accompany the *cante jondo*, as did regional variants such as the *fandango* from Cádiz and the *malagueña* from Málaga. Similarly, the *sevillana* was a medieval country dance appropriated by flamenco.

While traditionalists bemoan the commercialisation of flamenco, the spirit of *duende* has moved on, and probably into the hands of a performer such as Enrique Morente. Morente has pushed the envelope of flamenco more than anyone, producing flamenco masses, working with improvising jazz groups, even delving into electronics and avant-garde sound with bands such as fellow Granadinos Largartija Nick.

Inevitably, flamenco has crossed over with rock and dance music, to the chagrin of purists. Yet to anyone who has observed the dissipation of other Mediterranean folk musics, such as Greek *syrtaki*, the success of bands such as Ketama and Radio Tarifa suggests that Spain's young are maintaining a powerful link with tradition that has simply been abandoned elsewhere.

Flamenco is as popular now as it ever was

# Festivals and Events

Three annual celebrations – the pre-Lenten Carnaval, Easter and Pentecost/Corpus Christi – vary in date as they are religious festivals. Carnaval (*see below*) also depends on the fall of Lent. Corpus Christi falls seven weeks after Easter.

Carnaval goers in Cádiz

Easter and the *Semana Santa* (holy week) is the biggest celebration of the year, nowhere more so than in Seville, where hotels book up six months ahead. Each neighbourhood has a *hermandade* ('brotherhood') which organises community processions.

**Fiesta de San Anton**
*16 January, Huéscar*
Massive firework display with a celebration of local cuisine.
*16–17 January, El Ejido, Almería*
Processions culminate in a vast bonfire.

Christmas lights in Seville's back streets

**Carnaval**
*February*
Cádiz's Carnaval is the oldest in Spain, with parades, parties, costumes and mischief. Most communities celebrate, although at a slightly more sedate pitch.

**Feria de las Cruzes**
*Last week in April, Córdoba*
Competition for the best floral decorations in the old town.

**National Festival of Flamenco**
*Last week in April–mid-May, Córdoba*
One of the biggest flamenco festivals in Spain, followed by Córdoba's fair and bullfighting festival.

**Feria de Patios**
*First week in May, Córdoba*
The old town opens its domestic patios.

**Feria de San Isidro**
*15 May, various sites*
Flower festivals, fertility rites and food celebrations.

**Feria del Caballo**
*Mid-May, Jerez de la Frontera*
Traders descend on the oldest country event and biggest animal fair in Andalucía.

**Romería el Rocio**
*Whitsun week, El Rocio*
The most famous religious pilgrimage in Andalucía, in which up to half a million pilgrims converge on this small town to

celebrate its miraculous icon of the Virgin.

**Corpus Christi**
*17 June, Zahara de la Sierra*
Zahara celebrates by cladding the entire town centre in living greenery for just one day.

**Romería de los Gitanos**
*Third weekend in June, Cabra*
Major *gitano* pilgrimage to the shrine of the Virgen de la Sierra.

**Candelas de San Juan**
*23 June, Vejer de la Frontera*
Bonfires and a giant pyrotechnic bull illuminate this white village.

**Festival Internaciónal de Música y Danza de la Cueva de Nerja**
*July*
Month-long festival of classical and popular concerts by world-class performers in the town's remarkable cave system.

Seville's elegant Museo de Bellas Artes

**Fiesta de la Virgen del Carmen**
*16 July, Marbella*
The image of the Virgin is carried to the harbour where boats accompany her to Puerto Banus and back.

**International Festival of Arts**
*Last two weeks in July, Jimena de la Frontera*
For its modest size, this pretty town attracts impressive classical, jazz and popular music names.

**Musica en la Juderia**
*Whole of August, Córdoba*
Concerts in historic buildings around the old town.

**Feria de Málaga**
*Second week in August*
The liveliest feria in the province.

**Feria del la Virgen de Mar**
*Last fortnight of August, Almería*
Parades, open-air dances, sports, flamenco and concerts, plus a closing firework display.

**Exaltación al Rio Guadalquivir**
*Last two weekends in August, Sanlúcar de Barrameda*
Dramatic horse races, said to date back thousands of years, along a low-tide track on the beach, with landward celebrations in this town famed for its seafood and manzanilla sherry.

**La Goyesca**
*First week in September, Ronda*
Ronda's autumn fair closes with the Goyesca bullfight, fought in the costumes shown in Goya's paintings of bullfight scenes.

**Ferias**
*Throughout September*
Towns across Andalucía celebrate the traditional autumn fair, often staggered to allow towns to visit each other's festivities.

# Impressions of Seville

Seville is in many ways the perfect Spanish city: big enough
to boast some of the finest architectural monuments in the
country, but small enough to be easily negotiable on foot,
and with a compact street layout that is easy to memorise.
In the centre, the Giralda tower is a constant landmark,
and if you stray from the city centre then the curving rio
Guadalquivir or busy calle de Menendez Pelayo will steer
you back.

Seville's café culture

## Getting Around Seville

Unless you intend to explore the Expo
site or the depths of Triana across the
river, Seville is the ideal place to
abandon cars and taxis for some
incredible walks back through Spanish
history.

## When to Go

Spring and autumn are usually the best
times to visit Seville and Andalucía as a
whole, although a run of El Niño
summers has unbalanced the traditional
pattern of clement springs and autumns,
ferociously hot summers and temperate
winters. It can be balmy in mid-winter
and unexpectedly rainy in high summer,
although droughts are a regular
occurrence throughout Andalucía.

Easter's *Semana Santa*, or holy week,
and to a lesser extent the subsequent
April Fair, require stamina, a plump
purse or wallet and military planning.
Hotels book up as much as six months
in advance, room prices can triple and
some central hotels are so close to the
round-the-clock celebrations that sleep
is out of the question.

Summers in and around Seville,
situated in the 'frying pan' of Andalucía,
can be so hot that day-tripper traffic
actually withers back until the autumn,
making this a good time to visit if you
can handle the heat.

Otherwise spring, which can begin as
early as February, is the ideal time to
visit Seville and the region, although late
autumn and even mid-winter can
surprise with mild, sunny and even hot
days – but be prepared for the rains that
keep Andalucía so fertile. Layers of
clothing for hot days and cool nights are
best, and a light waterproof is always
good insurance.

## Driving

Spain is one of the most dangerous
driving environments in Europe, both in
the countryside and cities. Speed limits
exist everywhere – 60kph (37mph) in
cities and built-up areas, 90kph (55mph)
on other roads, 120kph (75mph) on
motorways – and although spot checks
are carried out daily drivers commonly
flout these limits. The N340, for
example, which girdles Andalucía's

The capital has rail links across Europe

coastline from Almería to Tarifa and north to Cádiz, is said to be the most dangerous road in Europe – for pedestrians and drivers alike.

If you have hired a car from Seville's San Pablo airport (or indeed are driving anywhere in Andalucía) it's advisable either to book ahead into a hotel with private parking or head for a secure car park. Street parking is a nightmare in Seville's warren of streets, and thefts from cars are a regular occurrence.

Commonsense security should apply wherever you park a car – in particular you should ensure that nothing valuable is left visible in your vehicle. Parking can be problematic in almost every other city and town in Andalucía (indeed, Spain as a whole), where centres were built hundreds of years before the invention of the combustion engine. Even townsfolk can spend ages driving around looking for somewhere to park.

In the centre of Granada, beware sections of some roads marked by low black poles with red lamps on top: these are automatically operated barriers to

allow residents-only access via swipe card. Look for signs saying *Obstaculos en calzada* giving the distance, and don't try jumping one: they're timed to open and close to allow just one car to pass.

**Getting Around**

There are frequent buses between airport and city centre, to and from the main rail terminus at Santa Justa just outside the centre, and long-distance connections throughout Andalucía and beyond. Seville has two main bus termini: Plaza de Armas, near the Puente de Cachorro bridge on the banks of the Guadalquivir, and at Prado de San Sebastiane on Avenida de Carlos V, a block away from the Jardines de Murillo. Armas buses head west and north, San Sebastiane buses south. Taxi drivers will often ask where you are going and head for the right bus station anyway.

The vast Santa Justa rail station has links to Madrid and on to northern Europe, as well as regional destinations such as Cádiz, Córdoba, Granada, Huelva, Málaga and beyond. As elsewhere in Spain, the RENFE rail network is cheap, clean, (usually) efficient, and can be used to get to most places around Andalucía. It is also the best way to see the country – the Bobadilla–Jimena de la Frontera route is generally regarded as one of the great mountain rail journeys of Europe. There are also some lesser known services in Andalucía, such as the five-hour high-speed journey from Algeciras to Madrid, or the overnight hotel train to Barcelona that leaves Málaga daily (9pm) and returns each morning. RENFE has an excellent website with route maps, times and prices, online booking and an English-language edition at *www.renfe.es*.

There is one crucial piece of advice for anyone leaving Seville (or any other large city or town) by train: like all major RENFE stations, Santa Justa operates a ticketed service system at its counters, with different tickets for different services (look for the press-button vending machines that dispense the numbered slips; numbers being served appear above specific counters). While democratic, this is also a lengthy process. Allow at least 30 minutes before departure to buy or collect your ticket(s). Missed trains are common among those unaware of the system – no fun if you have connections onwards or to other countries. Inter-city and international trains usually have ticket barriers and guards who will refuse entry to anyone without a ticket, although it's common to pay on board on shorter regional train services.

### Taxis

While some are dishonest, the vast majority of *taxistas*, taxi drivers, are scrupulously fair, and work to a meter and fixed charges for a list of destinations that drivers carry in their cab. Flat fares begin around €2 a kilometre, with a nominal extra per item of luggage in the boot, and premium fares kick in late at night and on festival days. Ask for an estimate – 'Cuanto cuesta?' ('How much?') – if unsure.

### Bikes

Pedal bikes, mopeds and motorcycles are available for hire in most towns and cities, although they are best left to experienced riders. Spanish two-wheel culture is as cavalier as its four-wheel culture, and neither is pedestrian-friendly. However, there are parts – notably the Costa de la Luz, Huelva region, the Guadalquivir, Guadiaro and Genal valleys, and Almería – where a bike, powered or otherwise, is the best form of transport.

### Banks and Credit Cards

Virtually all bank ATMs in Spain are international and will dispense euros against your home account, although not all banks will exchange foreign currency or travellers' cheques. Look for the *Cambio* (change) sign, ideally with a neighbouring *sin comisión* (no commission) notice.

Credit cards (Amex, Diners, Visa, Mastercard etc.) are widely accepted, although not always in smaller or independent hotels. Some smaller shops and restaurants are the same – the Spanish get round this by using charge cards that debit their accounts automatically.

Not all stores take credit cards

## Restaurants and Bars

The Spanish eat late: lunch is rarely before 2pm, dinner anything between 9pm and midnight or later. Traditionally lunch is the larger meal and dinner a light supper or tapas. Unless a bill stipulates otherwise, service is usually included, although it's considered polite to round up to the tidiest near figure. If you feel you've been well served or the food deserves special thanks, a tip of 10–15 per cent is sufficient.

Bars vary from tiny hole-in-the-wall kiosks to state-of-the-art designer cocktail joints. Food or a snack is considered an integral part of having a drink with friends, and many bars will serve a free tapas, unasked, with each drink, varied (meat, fish, cheese etc.) depending on the drink. Many will also have a tapas menu with prices. Prices at the bar are often different (cheaper) than table service, and some outdoor bars and restaurants will also charge extra for terrace service. Tipping is discretionary, and less common than in restaurants.

## Nightlife

The nocturnal behaviour of the Spanish can baffle even the long-term *guiri* (not very affectionate slang for a foreigner living in Spain). An evening with friends or at the cinema can be followed by a respite, or nap, before embarking on a (largely abstemious) round of bar- or club-hopping until the *madrugada* (small hours), or even until it is time to go to work. Few clubs will open before 11pm or midnight, most discotheques only really warm up around 2am or later, and most hip nightclubs will tell you not

to bother showing up until 4am. Most late night bars are free, and many nightclubs offer free entry early in the night, with prices (normally covering a first drink) rising as the night proceeds. In some city centre areas, clubs may operate dress codes against jeans and trainers. This could be a precaution, but it could also be a sign that the venue has a reputation for trouble.

## Women Travellers

While circumstances have changed drastically for women travellers in Spain, certain precautions remain advisable, particularly for the lone traveller. While a younger, educated, generation of males has been learning from its sisters, aunts and female contemporaries, women travelling without men are still considered a cultural anomaly. Women travelling together are sometimes assumed to be lesbian, which might actually work to your advantage. The commonsense precautions for any city or town – avoiding unlit and sparsely populated areas, dressing to avoid snatch thieves, declining unwanted attention politely but firmly, looking as if you know where you're going and so on – apply here as anywhere. It should also be borne in mind that Spain is still far safer than San Francisco, New York, London, Paris, Berlin, Athens and many another metropolis besides. Unusually, women travelling with babies or small children can expect the VIP treatment: the Spanish adore children, and hotels and restaurants go out of their way to welcome them. (Some 'boutique' hotels, however, do operate unofficial age limits, effectively barring children under, say, 12 or 15.)

## Gay and Lesbian Life

The *movida*, movement, of the post-Franco early 1980s triggered an avalanche of social changes, although largely in the cities. Women's rights, lesbian and gay rights and a whole raft of other emancipation movements were swept along by a wave of modernisation that had been held back since the 1960s.

The age of consent for gays and lesbians in Spain is 16, as across the EU. There are large lesbian and gay communities in Cádiz, Granada, Málaga, Seville and the beach resort of Torremolinos. There are often gender-specific bars and cafés, and nightclubs devoted to dress codes such as leather, but most are mixed and often quite popular with heterosexuals as well.

## Law

If you happen to encounter, or need the assistance of, Spain's legal system it is

Seville's vast Santa Justa rail station

best to note that it – or at least its public face – comes armed and isn't terribly friendly.

There are three distinct branches of law enforcement in Spain. The Guardia Civil wear combat-like green militaristic uniforms and have an unfortunate reputation based on their past notoriety as Franco's henchmen. Visitors will probably only encounter them operating spot-checks on motorways. However, in some rural areas, these may be the only law officers on duty.

The Policia Municipal wear a more sedate blue-and-white uniform and are more approachable than the GC. You should seek them or their offices out if you are robbed or mugged, or to report any serious physical or sexual assault. They are more likely to be sympathetic in serious cases and easier to deal with when seeking a crime report, which is essential if you intend to claim stolen property on an insurance policy.

The Policia Nacional in their natty brown riot-response type uniforms are normally only ever seen guarding events of state, controlling crowds and demonstrations, and outside sensitive sites such as embassies, ministry offices and military bases.

Although each of these is armed, the PN heavily so, most visitors to Spain probably won't even notice them. There are some circumstances, however, where forewarned could be forearmed.

*Identification*: Everyone in Spain, visitors included, is expected to carry some means of identification, and indeed the Spanish are bemused when visitors don't carry some form of ID. All Spanish citizens and residents carry a *residencia*, proof of residency, and NIE, or social security, card. Normally, these are only used to verify ID against credit card transactions. In theory, if you are stopped by the police and don't have ID on you, you can be spot-fined or even arrested and gaoled. Hotels will often keep passports briefly, to confirm identity, but should return them after verification.

*Nude or topless bathing*: Many resorts have designated nudist bathing beaches, and topless bathing is quite widespread on beaches in more developed resorts, but both are still technically forbidden. Take local advice on both, and be aware that what might be acceptable dress on the beach can cause offence away from it and in less sophisticated locales. The same applies to dressing to visit churches and other monuments.

*Drugs*: Spain's drug laws have been in a state of upheaval over the past decade or so. After a period of liberalisation, the signs are that the state's attitude towards drug use is hardening. Despite that, drugs are – perhaps because of Andalucía's proximity to north Africa – quite prevalent in Andalucía, even in small towns, and this includes Class A drugs such as cocaine and Ecstasy and its variants.

Possession of a 'personal use' amount of marijuana (affectionately nicknamed 'chocolate' in Spain) was decriminalised by the Socialist government in 1983. This was later rescinded, although in practice police have little time or inclination to pursue personal drug use. Things are very different when larger quantities are involved, and the police are likely to be harsher with *extranjeros*

(foreigners), found in possession of any quantity of drugs. Spain is under international pressure to render its borders less porous to any forms of smuggling – people, cigarettes and alcohol as much as drugs – and the spread of addiction among even rural communities has harshened people's attitudes to even the harmless *porro* (joint). In this climate, the visitor should consider dabbling in Spain's drug culture as very much AYOR – at your own risk.

## Consulates and Embassies

Most countries have consulates or representatives in the larger regional cities, and embassies in Madrid, who will assist or advise with robberies, loss or theft of passports, emergency repatriation, and so on. If arrested, you have the legal right to contact your consulate, although their willingness to become involved varies from country to country.

## Insurance

For Britons and other EU citizens the E111 form or its equivalent should smooth access to any necessary medical treatment in accident and emergency or outpatients' departments or at a medical centre. However, the advice to visitors from outside the EU – to take out a travel insurance policy with adequate health and repatriation cover – should also be taken seriously by EU residents. Some treatments and medications can only be obtained privately, and even under a health insurance scheme this will have to be paid for and claimed against the policy.

# Seville

Seville leaps out on the unwary first-time visitor. Approached from any direction, by car, bus or train, its skyline starts to bristle with modernist bridgespans, church spires and half-glimpsed monuments such as the Plaza de Toros, the Torre del Oro and, of course, La Giralda tower.

Torre del Oro

The city is a palimpsest of different historical eras and styles, as over the centuries layers of different cultures – Roman, Visigoth, Berber, Almohad, Mudéjar, Gothic, Renaissance, Baroque and, across the rio Gudalquivir, the alarming perspectives and colour-schemes of 20th-century post-modernism around the Expo 92 site – were imposed on earlier civilisations.

Parque de Maria Luisa

## Orientation

Standing in the Plaza de Triunfo with the Giralda to your right, Avenida de la Constitución ahead of you leads left towards the Parque María Luisa, its gardens and the magnificent tiled Plaza de España from the 1929 Exposition. En route it also passes the grand Hotel Alfonso XIII and the vast Fábrica de Tabácos, Mérimée and Carmen's tobacco factory, now the city university.

Take la Constitución right and it heads along the western edge of Santa Cruz, which as well as the Giralda and Alcázares also encompasses the Jardines de Murillo, the Ayuntamiento (city council) and the beautiful Casa de Pilatos.

Across the Avenida from Santa Cruz is El Arenal, stretching to the river and boasting the riverside Torre del Oro, the exquisite

Museo de Bellas Artes and, between them, the rather more modern Plaza de Toros bullring and its neighbour, the world-class Teatro de la Maestranza opera house and theatre.

The scruffiest of the *barrios*, northernmost La Macarena, is also perhaps where the soul of Seville can be found. This traditional family district is home to perhaps the most potent symbol of the city, the statue of the Virgen de la Esperanza Macarena, the most revered of all the religious statuary in the city and the one most likely to inspire mass hysteria on her irregular appearances in the street (*see pp46–7*).

Thus oriented, the next thing the visitor should do is get spectacularly, hopelessly lost. Its monuments may be the shop window of the city, but the spirit of Seville is in the street life lived by the Sevillanos in those warrens of back streets, alleys and plazas, which often conceal little-visited gems.

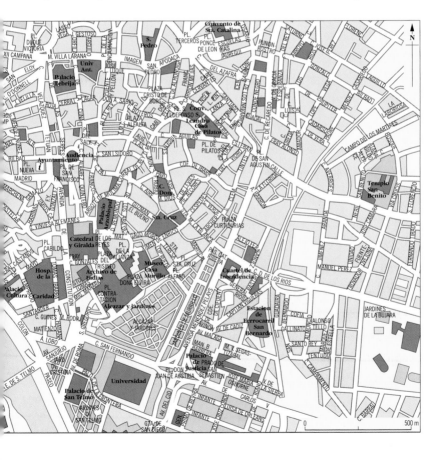

# Reales Alcázares

Andalucíans and visitors alike are split over the charms of Seville's Alcázar (fortress) compared to those of its nearest rival, Granada's Alhambra and Generalife gardens. The Alcázar is smaller and more enclosed than the rambling open-air Alhambra, which perhaps gives its courtyards, halls and spectacular decor an intensity lacking in Granada's hilltop monument.

There has been a structure on the site of the Alcázar since Roman times, and palatial accommodation for royalty since the 14th century. It became a fort for the Córdoban caliphate in the 10th century and was expanded by Almohad rulers in the 12th century. Following the reconquest of Seville, King Pedro I, known as Pedro the Cruel to history but Pedro the Just to his cronies, began a programme of expansion that continued sporadically over the centuries.

## Patio del León

The Puerta del León, the entrance to the Alcázar, leads through original Almohad walls to the Patio del León courtyard, where Pedro dispensed summary justice after deliberating in the neighbouring **Sala de la Justicia**. Just off the Sala is the exquisite **Patio del Yeso**, a small multi-arched water garden with Almohad designs dating from the 12th century.

## Patio de la Monteria

This larger open-air patio, where the court would gather before hunting expeditions, is dominated by the entrance to the Palacio de Pedro I, which gives a hint of the architectural glories to come. The multi-levelled balconied façade is a prime example of the rhythmic patterning of Mudéjar architecture.

## Palacio de Pedro I

The upper levels of the Palacio remain the property of the Spanish monarchy even today: King Juan Carlos I has apartments here, where his daughter Elena celebrated her marriage in 1995.

At the heart of the Palacio sits the **Patio de las Doncellas**, the Patio of the Maidens, whose galleried upper floor gives on to a variety of private salons built at various stages in the Palacio's history. Here, in the minutely detailed plasterwork originally fashioned by hand by craftsmen from Granada, the visitor

can take a measure of the extraordinary efforts that went into constructing this perfect space intended for the eyes of only a select few. The work that created this perfect symmetry would have taken years.

This effect increases in the neighbouring **Patio de las Muñecas**, the Patio of the Dolls (after two small faces to be found in one of its arches), where the arithmetical repetitions of

pattern are enhanced by the strong use of *azulejos* (glazed tiling) on the walls. This in turn leads on to the Alcázar's crowning glory, the **Salón de Embajadores**, the 15th-century Ambassadors' Hall, whose stunning domed ceiling, made of interlocking pieces of gilded wood, still dazzles today. It is a masterpiece of design from a culture where representational art was strictly forbidden (*see pp44–5*).

### Salones de Carlos V
Things quieten down a little after the Ambassadors' Hall. The Salones de Carlos V were remodelled in the 16th century within an original 13th-century Gothic palace and today house a collection of historic tapestries hung beneath a magnificent vaulted ceiling.

### Jardines de la Alcázar
The gardens beyond were originally laid out in the 12th century but are today seen in 16th-century form. The gardens, a symmetrical jungle of towering palms and pines criss-crossed by water courses and studded with fountains, have to be the most placid spot in the whole of Seville. *Tel: 954 50 23 23. Open: Mon–Sat 9.30am–5pm, Sun 9.30am–1.30pm. Admission charge.*

Facing page: Gardens designed for intrigues
Above: Mudéjar arches in the Palacio del Pedro I
Left: The elegant Patio del Yeso at the heart of the Alcázar

# Santa Cruz

Catedral entrance

The former Jewish quarter is the liveliest and most historically charged of all Seville's *barrios*. As well as the Reales Alcázares and the cathedral (*see pp36–7*) it also encompasses the Archivo de Indias, the 16th-century repository of documents relating to Spain's conquest of meso-America, the exquisite 17th-century Hospital de los Venerables Sacerdotes, the Jardines de Murillo and the Museo de Arte Contemporáneo.

Of equal interest is the **cultural life** of this busiest of the *barrios*. Starting on calle Mateos Gagos, leading off the northeast corner of the Plaza del Triunfo, Santa Cruz's scrambled streets and alleys conceal some of Seville's finest bars and restaurants, and not a few of its best hotels as well. Most nights of the week and most weeks of the year, its bars and restaurants are thronged with Sevillanos and visitors who have stumbled on this carelessly kept secret.

### Archivo de Indias

At the 'bottom' of the Plaza del Triunfo (*see opposite*), this was originally built as a stock exchange to conduct Seville's crucial role as 'office' of the Spanish Americas. In 1785 it was converted into an archive dedicated to collecting documents relating to the colonial enterprise, and is nowadays said to house over 80 million pages of documents, most only available to scholars.
*Plaza del Triunfo. A small museum (open: Mon–Fri 10am–1pm; free) rotates exhibits related to the archive.*

### Callejón del Agua

No visit to Santa Cruz would be complete without a walk along the pedestrianised Callejón del Agua, a narrow alley running beneath the Alcazar garden walls and into the heart of the *barrio*.

### Casa de Pilatos

This house was built in the 16th century by the first Marquess of Tarifa as a palatial storeroom for the artworks he gathered on his journeys around Europe and to the Holy Land. Subsequent occupants maintained the tradition and today the Casa rivals the Alcázar in its architectural splendour and the treasures it contains.
*Calle Águilas. Open: daily 9am–7pm. Admission charge.*

### Hospital de los Venerables Sacerdotes

*Open: daily 10am–2pm & 2–4pm. Closed: Aug. Guided tours only. Admission charge.*

## Jardines de Murillo

Plaza Santa Cruz, one of the oldest
(1692) and prettiest of the *barrio*'s
squares, gives on to these slender
public gardens, named after the painter
Bartolomé Murillo (1618–82) who lived
in nearby calle Santa Teresa, where his
former house is now a museum. The
gardens feature a towering monument
to Columbus.

*Gardens open: sunrise–sunset. Museo de
Murillo, calle Santa Teresa. Open:
Tue–Sun 10am–2pm & 5–9pm. Free.*

Columbus monument, Jardines de Murillo

## Museo de Arte Contemporáneo

This museum was moved into the Plaza
del Triunfo from nearby calle Santo
Tomas in the 1990s. It is one of the
few spaces in Seville where you can see
regional and national contemporary art,
often at its most combative.

*Plaza del Triunfo. Open: Mon–Fri
10am–1pm. Free.*

## Plaza del Triunfo

It is unlikely that any other Spanish city
can match the historic convergence
around this plaza. Each side of the
square has at least one building of major
cultural importance. The central statue
of the Immaculate Conception is a
latter-day addition to a monument built
to acknowledge the city's survival of the
devastating Lisbon earthquake of 1755.

One wall of the Plaza del Triunfo is
occupied by the façade of the 18th-
century **Palacio Arzobispal**, across the
Plaza Virgin de los Reyes by the entrance
to La Giralda; the palace is still used by
the church authorities and is not open to
the public. The **Plaza Virgin de los Reyes**
is one of the key stopping points for
La Macarena's regular perambulations
of the city, when crowds flock to glimpse
the Virgin's candlelit bier leaving the
cathedral.

# Catedral and La Giralda

Seville's cathedral and great bell tower La Giralda sit on the site of a mosque built by Almohad invaders who reached the city in 1147 and set about building the tower and the riverside Torre del Oro. When the Christians took Seville back in 1428, they converted the mosque into a Christian church and began the first of a series of alterations to the tower, starting with its Moorish dome and pinnacle. Today, the Moorish base is capped by a Renaissance belfry housing its fearsome carillon and topped by La Giralda weathervane, the figure of Faith astride the globe.

Capilla Mayor

## Catedral

The mosque-church was demolished at the start of the 15th century in favour of a brand new cathedral to accompany the tower. It took over a hundred years to build and when completed was said to be the largest Gothic church in the world. More recent calculations of its floor plan and volume suggest that it may in fact be the largest church in the world.

## Capilla Mayor

The most remarkable feature of this church crammed with marvels is the Capilla Mayor, or main altar, dominated by a vast *retablo* (altar-piece) featuring 45 scenes from the life of Christ. As befits the biggest church on the planet, this is also the planet's biggest altar-piece, the life-work of one artist, Pierre Dancart.

## Iglesia del Sagrario

This smaller church to the left of the entrance to the nave dates from the 17th century and is nowadays used as a parish church serving the local community.

## Patio de los Naranjos

The iglesia opens out into a curiosity in a Christian church: the Patio de los Naranjos, a handsome large courtyard lined with symmetrically planted orange trees. The space dates from the site's period as a mosque, and is where Moorish worshippers would have washed hands and feet in the central fountain before entering the mosque.

## Tomb of Columbus

To the right of the vast Capilla Mayor is a small chapel containing the tomb installed in 1890 to house the remains of Columbus, which had been transported here from Cuba. His coffin is supported by four carved figures representing the royal houses of Castilla, León, Aragón and Navarra.

## Sacristia Mayor

Beyond the tomb, the Sacristia Mayor contains a collection of paintings by Murillo, and a sizeable collection of still more jewelled and gold-bound religious artefacts.

## La Giralda

The Giralda tower underwent no fewer than four major changes in design in the first 400 years of its existence, finally reaching the shape we see today in 1568. It is recommended especially to anyone who has found themselves mountaineering giddily up into the extremities of similar Gothic edifices in Cologne and Siena. La Giralda was built so that two mounted guards could patrol as far up as its belfry. As both men and their mounts needed a shallow gradient, a set of wide and gentle stairs spirals up towards the belfry, which affords magnificent 360 degree views out across the city.

*Catedral & Giralda open: Mon–Sat 11am–5pm, Sun 2–7pm. Admission charge. Times may vary: tel: 954 21 49 71 for details.*

Seville's Catedral and La Giralda tower seen from the Plaza del Triunfo

No one forgets their first encounter with a *nazareno*, the hooded and cloaked penitents (*nazarenos*) who form the processions that fill the streets of Seville and every other Spanish city and town during Easter. Accompanied by brass bands and lavishly decorated *pasos* (biers), carrying statues of the Virgin Mary and scenes from the Passion, the figures in their Klan-like disguises can strike terror in the unwitting spectator, and need some explaining.

The marches by local *hermandades* or *cofradias* (brotherhoods) date back as far as the 14th century and the Reconquest. The form they take today dates from the 17th century, when

many of the sumptuous, larger-than-life statues of the Virgin and scenes from Christ's last days (roughly from Gethsemane to Golgotha) were first fashioned. The costumes, which were indeed copied by the USA's Ku Klux Klan for their scare factor, actually come from the anonymous robes of the Spanish Inquisition. At night, lit by braziers, the sight of the *nazarenos* weighed down in their panoply and accompanied by barefoot penitents in chains and rags dragging life-sized crosses behind them, can resemble a tableau from a Gothic horror film. Yet these are largely seen as neighbourhood get-togethers and involve women as well as men, young people and even children. Membership of a *hermandad* is a much sought-after privilege, even by those who wouldn't normally see the inside of a church at any other time of the year.

The routes taken by the *pasos* weave through the streets from each *hermandad*'s local church towards the cathedral, and the further away the church – such as the Basilica de la Macarena – the longer the march: some can be on the streets for 12 hours. The biers can be heavy: depending on their size they can require anything between 40 and 90 bearers, working in relays and swaying in rhythm to displace the weight of the bier. The biers, *nazarenos* and community brass bands are interspersed with groups of local dignitaries and led by a *capataz*, or

captain, who rings a bell to announce regular rest breaks, or sometimes just to let stragglers catch up.

Despite the solemn nature of the marches and the events for which they are atoning, the mood on the pavements is usually celebratory, especially so on Good Friday morning (Thursday from midnight, in fact), which is the climax of the week. (Processions continue until Easter Sunday, although these are less spectacular and thinly attended.) The Thursday daytime processions are sombre affairs, where visitors are asked not to dress in shorts and T-shirts out of respect, but otherwise the atmosphere is one of a long street party. The crowning moment is usually the arrival of La Macarena at the cathedral, usually around 6am on Friday, when even an *ateo* (atheist) might feel moved by the Virgin, resplendent in her jewelled gowns and carried aloft on a bier decked with flowers and ablaze with candlelight.

While few other Semana Santa celebrations approach the intensity of those in Seville, almost every town and village will have its processions with the statue of the local Virgin Mary and scenes from the Passion. Tourist offices and local newspapers publish timetables and routes for each *hermandad*'s processions through the week.

Facing page: *Nazarenos* (hooded and cloaked penitents) in one of Seville's solemn Easter marches
Above: Easter Saturday is a time to recuperate

# El Arenal

This historic *barrio*, between the Avenida de la Constitución and the río Guadalquivir, can claim to be one of the oldest areas of the city. Before the Guadalquivir began to silt up in the 16th century, making it impossible for seagoing craft to reach Seville by the early 17th century, the site of El Arenal ('quicksand' in one translation) was the city's port and the hub of Spain's maritime commerce with the rest of the world.

Plaza de Toros, Seville

Both Columbus and Magellan sailed from here, their sails visible for miles across the flat tidal plains of the Guadalquivir valley. El Arenal's maritime importance stretches further back, however, to the 12th-century Almohad invasion, when the Moors initiated the construction of both the Giralda tower and the Torre del Oro.

### Hospital de la Caridad

El Arenal is inadvertently responsible for producing a quasi-mythic figure who himself inspired operas and drama, Don Juan. The 17th-century playboy-turned-philanthropist Miguel de Mañara is claimed by some to be the model for notorious seducer Don Juan Tenorio. Yet it was Mañara who founded the charitable **Hospital de la Caridad**, still in use today to care for the elderly and infirm. Its chapel contains a small but vibrant collection of paintings by Murillo, Leal and others.
*Calle Temprado. Open: Mon–Sat 9am–1.30pm & 3.30–7.30pm, Sun 9am–1pm. Admission charge.*

### Museo de Bellas Artes

This secular masterpiece lies at the northernmost edge of El Arenal. A former convent, the building now houses one of the finest collections of Spanish art under one roof, ranging from medieval to 20th-century but concentrating on the heyday of the 'Seville School' from the 15th century, in particular the works of Murillo, Zurbarán and Leal. The 16th-century convent building, built around three beautiful courtyards and crammed with interior details such as the domed ceiling of its Baroque gallery, is worth a visit in itself.
*Plaza del Museo. Open: Tue 3–8pm, Wed–Sat 9am–8pm, Sun 9am–2pm. Admission charge (EU citizens free).*

### Plaza de Toros de la Maestranza

The presence of a large, Baroque-fronted white bullring on this plaza, equidistant between the Torre del Oro and Museo de Bellas Artes, suggests another strand to the cultural history of El Arenal. In the centuries when the *barrio* sat between the fortified Alcázar walls and the

El Arenal and La Giralda seen from Triana

dockyards, this was a lively seaport district. Many of the city's famous bars and restaurants were situated here and some, such as the Bodegón Torre del Oro on calle Santander, remain. Similarly, the streets off Garcia de Vinuesa, off la Constitución, conceal marvellous *fino* bars (*see p54*) and fish restaurants.

### Teatro de la Maestranza

Culture of a more rarefied kind arrived on the riverbank across the paseo de Cristóbal Colón in 1991 with the opening of the Teatro de la Maestranza. This world-class opera house and concert hall was conceived to usher in the 1992 Expo and is home to the Orquesta Sinfónica de Seville, regularly hosting touring opera, dance, concert and drama performances.
*Paseo de Cristóbal Colón. For bookings tel: 954 22 33 44.*

### Torre del Oro

This tower was originally a watchtower built into the defensive walls that surrounded the Alcázar and the city centre. It was taken back in the Reconquest less than 100 years later, and in the 15th century the tower was used to store bounty brought back from the Americas. Today it houses a modest maritime museum and is the place to find pleasure cruisers moored nearby for trips along the riverbank and downriver to Sanlúcar de Barrameda and the Coto Doñana wildlife reserve.
*Torre del Oro, Paseo de Cristobal Colón. Open: Tue–Fri 10am–2pm, Sat–Sun 11am–2pm. Admission charge.*
*Cruceros Turisticos operate hourly river trips (lasting 1hr), daily 11am–10pm. Tel: 954 56 16 92. Admission charge.*

# Walk: Triana

A walk through the historic *barrio* of Triana across the river from El Arenal is more about capturing the spirit of a place than visiting great monuments – you left those behind as you walked across the Puente de Isabel II (also known as the Puente de Triana). For centuries, Triana was the *gitano* (gypsy) *barrio*, the mythic birthplace of flamenco, and also, coincidentally, the city's pottery district, a craft maintained to this day in its numerous *azulejo* (tiling) workshops.

*Allow 2 hours.*

### 1 Capillita del Carmen

The walk begins on the very perimeter of Triana, at the Triana side of the Puente de Isabel II. The curious *azulejo*-clad structure on the right hand is the Capillita del Carmen, a miniature chapel built in 1926. Diagonally opposite the Capillita is Triana's most famous *freiduría* (fried fish restaurant), the Kiosko de las Flores.

*Capillita del Carmen. Open: daily 9am–1pm & 5.30–9pm. Free.*

The Puente de Isabel II, or Triana Bridge

### 2 Calle San Jorge

Take calle San Jorge on the right to plunge into the pottery district, noting particularly the stores on calles Antillano Campos and Covadonga.

*Turning left onto Pages del Corro and then left at San Jacinto, Triana's main thoroughfare, you find calle Rodrigo de Triana on the first right.*

### 3 Calle Rodrigo de Triana

Named after the sailor who first sighted the New World on Columbus's first trip in 1492, Rodrigo is a typical Triana street, with a view of your next destination, the Iglesia de Santa Ana, above its rooftops.

### 4 Iglesia de Santa Ana

The dense warren of streets between San Jacinto and the iglesia is where Triana's displaced Roma population lived around communal courtyards, particularly on calle de Pelay Correa. The church was founded in the

13th century and is said to be the oldest parish church in Seville.
*Open: daily 9am–1pm & 5.30–9pm. Free. From the iglesia, walk east towards the river. Either take the calle de la Pureza northwards towards the tiny **Capilla de los Marineros**, the 18th-century sailors' chapel (open: daily 9am–1pm & 5.30–9pm; free), or continue to the riverfront and walk north along the calle Betis back towards the Puente de Isabel II.*

## 5 Calle Betis

The true spirit of Triana is best discovered by indulging in an aimless drift through its streets before coming to rest at an outdoor table on calle Betis. The stretch of the Guadalquivir below is one of the busiest stretches of the river. In all but the most inclement weather, it is popular with water sports *aficionados*, canoeists, small dinghy sailors and racing crews, and the bars and restaurants are the best places to watch their races and regattas.

*The calle Betis riverfront can also be pursued beyond the barrio centre as far as the Plaza de Cuba and the Puente de San Telmo, which leads across the river to the Puerta de Jerez and the Alcázar.*

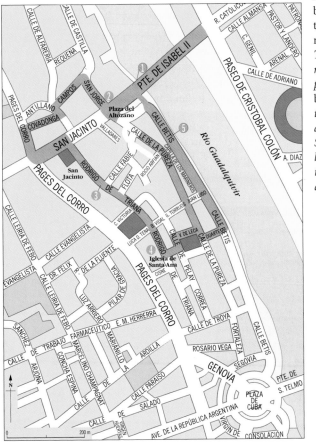

Seville's architecture, like the architecture of other great Andalucían cities such as Córdoba, represents an encyclopaedia of styles imported by invaders across the centuries. Several cultures – Visigoth, Moorish Berber, Almoravid and Almohad – were incorporated into an architecture known as Mudéjar. Later, north European Gothic, Renaissance and Baroque flourishes would be added to this mutant form.

Mudéjar itself is a hybrid word, from the Arabic *Mudajjan*, meaning 'those allowed to stay'. This refers both to those Moors who were allowed to convert to Christianity and remain in Spain after the Reconquest, and also a style of architecture that borrows from previous schools of design.

The classical Moorish arch, as seen in the Mezquita at Córdoba, was taken

from a pattern used in church design by the Visigoths. This was mixed with increasingly elaborate stucco work and the use of religious texts as decorative detail.

Later invaders, such as the Almohads, introduced more formal Islamic styles, such as those seen in La Giralda tower in Seville with its Moorish base and 15th-century Renaissance belfry. The later Nasrid invaders would become responsible for the extraordinary Alhambra and Generalife gardens, while the Mudéjar builders of the Reales Alcázares in Seville borrowed from a variety of designs.

Typically, and bearing in mind the length of time many of these buildings took to complete, or the tendency of later generations to alter, erase or replace earlier structures, some of the larger sites, such as the Alcázar and the Alhambra, represent a mixture of styles. Occasionally these would be used asynchronously, out of the 'order' in which these styles proceeded. A notable example of this is the Mudéjar Palacio Pedro I, which while Mudéjar in execution is almost entirely Moorish in style – a case, perhaps, of the builders quoting earlier styles to achieve a specific effect.

In almost every era of architecture employed in Moorish Spain, certain features remained constant: air, light, water and space. Running water, rarely very far away in any Moorish or Mudéjar

Facing page: Mudéjar arches overlooking the garden
Left: The rhythmic patterns of Arabic design are derived from mathematics
Below: Almería's handsome Alcazaba fortress, above the old town

decrepitude in the latter half of the 20th century.

A greater irony, perhaps, is that where later architectural schools contained homages to or pastiches of earlier styles, it would take an entirely different region of Spain to celebrate Mudéjar and similar styles. While Andalucía abandoned Moorish design to history, late 19th-century Barcelona's *modernistas* (modernists) such as Antoni Gaudí i Cornet and Lluis Domenech i Montaner, adapted Mudéjar – not least its stucco crenellations, rhythmic patterning and use of tiles – for their own dazzling designs.

structure, acted as air conditioning, ionised and cleared air, and aided meditation. Light was mediated through arched galleries and filigree screens such as the Almohad arches of the Patio del Yeso in the Alcázar. Space was kept in proportion but rarely stinted, as the Alhambra, rambling over what is in fact a foothill of the Sierra Nevada mountains, attests.

Two ironies attend the history of Moorish architecture in Spain. While some aspects were assimilated into later styles, the Reconquest set in train a programme of cultural vandalism that saw Moorish masterpieces destroyed or abandoned. Some monuments, such as the Moorish Palacio Mondragon in Ronda, were still languishing in

# La Macarena

Seville's northernmost *barrio* may lack the monumental attractions of its neighbours, but this largest of all districts is home to the Andalucían parliament, the few remaining sections of defensive Almohad walls, the most colourful street market in Seville and the most famous icon in the city, and perhaps in the whole of Spain: La Macarena.

Torre de Don Fadrique

On a more prosaic note, the corner of La Macarena near the Alameda de Hercules is one of the logical points for those on foot to venture across the river towards the Isla Mágica theme park and the sprawling Expo site (*see pp48–9*). Some older city maps feature a cable car to the park from near the Estacion de Córdoba. The cable car hasn't worked in years, and is unlikely to do so in the near future.

## Basilica de la Macarena

La Macarena and her *barrio* are believed to take their name from the Roman goddess Macaria, daughter of Hercules.

Icon of La Macarena

Her full title is the Virgen de la Esperanza Macarena – *esperanza* for hope, and a hope fulfilled: the tears on her doll-like cheeks are in grief at the death of her son.

Today the statue that can make grown men sob and rend their clothes can be viewed every day at the modern Basilica de la Macarena. As befits the most adored icon in Seville, the modest church is crammed with lavish votary artefacts – jewels, garments and other finery – donated by grateful supplicants. *Calle Macarena. Open: daily 9.30am–1pm & 5–9pm. Free.*

## Parish Churches

What it may lack in grand palaces, La Macarena more than compensates for with its handsome parish churches, not least the Iglesias de **Santa Catalina**, de **San Marcos**, de **Santa Paula** and de **San Pedro**, all, without exception, on their own eponymous Plazas (San Pedro is on calle Doña Maria Coronel). Built or remodelled at various stages in the Mudéjar, Gothic, Renaissance and Baroque periods, they all seem to allude to La Giralda visible on the horizon to the south.

*Churches open: daily 9.30am–1pm &
5–9pm.*

## Parlamento de Andalucía
Diagonally north of the Basilica de la
Macarena is the district's most historic
secular building. Previously known as
the 15th-century Hospital de las Cinco
Llagas, hospital of five wounds, the
Renaissance building was converted into
the parliament building in 1992. At the
time of construction it was the largest
hospital in Europe, and still treated
patients as recently as the 1960s.
*Plaza de la Macarena. Not open regularly
to the public, but guided tours are possible
by arrangement. Tel: 954 59 21 00. Free.*

The Macarena in all her splendour

## Street Markets
As befits a busy local neighbourhood,
La Macarena has its fair share of street
markets, notably **El Jueves** (Thursday)
on calle de la Feria, thought to be the
oldest street market in Seville. A few
blocks east of the Torre de Don
Fadrique, the wide **Alameda de
Hercules**, built in the 16th century for
the wealthy of Seville's Golden Age to
promenade, nowadays hosts the city's
biggest *rastro*, flea market, every Sunday
morning.

## Torre de Don Fadrique
A short walk away from the Plaza de
la Macarena, close to the Puente de
la Barqueta bridge – the one resembling
a strung bow laid lengthwise across the
river – is the other historic site in
La Macarena. The Torre de Don
Fadrique (*currently closed to the public*)
on calle Santa Clara is all that remains
of a 13th-century tower built as part of
a palace for the Infante Don Fadrique,
who would later meet a grisly end at the
hands of Pedro the Cruel's henchmen
in the Alcázar. The tower is now part of
the Convento de Santa Clara, secreted
in a lovely orange-lined courtyard, with
views across the river and south to
La Giralda.

Between April and October 1992, an estimated 36 million people visited the vast Expo 92 on La Isla de Cartujas (the 'island of the Carthusians') across the Guadalquivir from La Macarena. The site takes its name from the Carthusian monastery set back from the riverbank near the Pasarela la Cartuja footbridge built for the Expo. The monastery, used as a pottery until the 1960s, was itself extensively renovated for the Expo. *Monasterio de la Cartuja, Avenida Américo Vespucio. Open: Tue–Fri 10am–9pm, Sat 11am–9pm, Sun 10am–3pm. Admission charge (free to EU citizens).*

Despite continuing arguments over the cost and the fate of the site – much of it is still closed, or simply abandoned – there is little doubt that it put Seville, and Andalucía, higher up the list of

must-visit destinations than it had been for some years previously. It was also only one of four 20th-century Expo events judged a success, along with Brussels 58, Montreal 67 and Osaka 70.

Many of the international pavilions were dismantled after the Expo closed, while others, in the face of funding problems, have been absorbed into the Isla Mágica theme park. Still others, such as the Omnimax cinema, Parque Cientifico y Tecnologico and the Pabellón de los Discubrimientos (Pavilion of Discoveries) have operated as independent attractions but are temporarily closed. A large chunk of the Expo site has also been taken over by the University of Seville.

Approaching Seville by air, road, rail or river, it is impossible to ignore the drastic contrast between the two sides of the rio Guadalquivir here. A mere hundred yards from the medieval city, the tall blue cylinder of the 17-storey Pabellón de Andalucía leans away from the river at an alarming angle. A multi-storey outdoor lift-shaft soars into mid-air next to a defunct cable-car system. Futuristic pavilions loom on the central rectangle of the Parque Cientifico, its wide lateral boulevards named after Darwin, Einstein, Curie, Newton and Edison. Downriver, the huge dome of the Omnimax dwarfs a life-size model of Magellan's *Não Victoria*, the ship on which he circumnavigated the globe. Upriver, Santiago Calatrava's gravity-defying cantilevered Puente del Alamillo bridge leans out across the Guadalquivir. Inside and outside the Isla Mágica, volcanoes, space rockets, waterfalls and pirate ships add even more incongruous details to jostle with the antiquities just across the water.

Political controversy has dogged the Expo site ever since its inception, and several of its attractions, such as the Isla Mágica (née Parque Temático), have had to be bailed out financially and relaunched by the authorities, despite attracting large summer crowds to their white knuckle rides and themed history experiences. It is unlikely that these financial problems will be resolved in the short-term future.

However, the amount of publicity Seville as a city and Andalucía as a whole garnered during the Expo, while unquantifiable against the final, billions of pesetas outlay, was remarkable. Barely ten years after Spain had reinstated democracy, the Expo saw city, region and indeed Spain itself embracing modernity. It may have only been symbolic, but after centuries of *latifundismo* and a creeping tendency to regard itself as one big real-life theme park, Spain was at last striding into the future.

*Getting there: take buses C1 or C2 from Prado de San Sebastian bus station, Avenida de Málaga, opposite Jardines de Murillo.*

*Isla Magica open: 11am–11pm daily Apr–Sept, weekends only Oct–Mar. Admission charge.*

Seville's Expo and modernist architecture put it back on the map in 1992

Carmona's Puerta de
Sevilla

# Around Seville

It was only natural that, following the conquest of the
Americas, Seville's wealth should spill over into the
surrounding towns and villages. Seville's eastern flank,
towards Córdoba, boasts some of the most beautiful towns
in this part of Andalucía.

## Carmona

Its proximity to Seville, combined with
a wealth of architectural features and a
number of excellent hotels, make this an
ideal alternative to staying in Seville.
With a regular (hourly) bus service
(*40 mins*) into the centre of Seville, it's
also an attractive option for drivers
nervous of the capital's streets and
reputation for auto crime. At the heart
of its warren of medieval streets, the
Plaza de San Francisco is possibly the
loveliest square in the whole of
Andalucía.

Carmona has been inhabited since
pre-Christian Iberian times. Following
the Reconquest, it became a country
residence for King Pedro I (Pedro the
Cruel), architect of parts of the Reales
Alcázares and the castle that is now
Carmona's *parador*. The Roman
presence is preserved today, if only in
the fascinating Necrópolis and vestigial
auditorium on the outskirts. The town
museum and several churches, including
San Pedro, with a tower copied from the
Giralda, record later architectural and
cultural details.

### Museo de la Ciudad

Housed in an 18th-century mansion, the
town museum has a good collection of

artefacts from key eras in the history of
the town: prehistoric, Iberian, Roman,
Moorish and Christian, including pieces
from the Necrópolis.
*Calle San Ildefonso. Open: 10am–2pm &*
*6–9pm. Admission charge.*

### Necrópolis Romana

Discovered in 1868, this partially
excavated Roman burial site has so far
revealed a handful of family tombs,
communal crematoria and ossuaries, a
villa-like tomb for the daughter of a
local ruler and a mausoleum-temple
dedicated to the worship of Cybele and
Attis. Guided tours (*30 mins*) every
20 minutes.
*Calles Enmedio/Attis. Open: June–Sept*
*Mon–Sat 9am–2pm & Sun 10am–2pm;*
*Oct–Apr Mon–Sat 9am–2pm & Sun*
*11am–1.45pm. Free.*

### Écija

Possibly the hottest town in Spain, at the
heart of *la sartenilla* (the frying pan),
Écija is an architectural oddity. A total of
eleven 15th- and 16th-century church
towers dominate its old town centre,
a measure, along with its impressive
mansions, of Écija's wealth during the
Golden Age and its position at the
centre of the olive oil industry. The

churches and towers are currently in various states of disrepair, and the town's history can be traced in the Museo Historico Municipal.
*Museo Historico Municipal, calle Castillo. Open: Tue–Fri 9.30am–1.30pm & 4.30–6.30pm, Sat–Sun 9am–2pm. Free.*

**Osuna**

Built on a small mount in the plains east of Seville, Osuna is another cluster of fine Renaissance mansions topped by a trio of remarkable religious buildings. The lively Plaza Mayor and neighbouring calle San Pedro are the best places to see the (private) mansions, most accessibly the Palacio de los Marquesas de la Gomera, now a five-star hotel.

Clustered above the town are the Colegiata de Santa Maria, the Convento de la Encarnación and the Antigua Universidad. Only the first two are open to the public.
*Situated on the hill above the town. Colegiata & Convento open: Mon–Sat 10am–1.30pm & 4–7pm, Sun 10am–1.30pm. Admission charge.*

Osuna's hub, the busy Plaza Mayor with the town's casino (left) and *Ayuntamiento* – town council – (right)

# Jerez de la Frontera

Jerez is the quintessential Andalucían town, the home to *fino* ('dry') sherry and to a *gitano* flamenco culture second only to Seville, and the birthplace of classical, horseback, bullfighting, still practised today in its bullring. It is also very British, thanks to the presence of sherry dynasties such as Harvey, Williams & Humbert, Domecq, González Byass, Sandeman and others.

Jerez's imposing Alcázar

There has been a human settlement on the site of Jerez since Phoenician times. The Romans named it Xeres, the Moors Scheris, from which both *jerez* (Spanish for sherry) and sherry derive. The dry white fortified wines produced from the grapes of its temperate vineyards made it the leader of the three key sherry producing towns in Andalucía (*see pp52–3*). The sherry trade also made its sherry dynasties extremely wealthy, a wealth reflected in the monuments and great houses of the town's centre.

Being so close to the great port of Cádiz, it is perhaps unsurprising that Jerez is also a notably industrialised town. The town centre, however, as elegant as Seville itself, conceals numerous architectural delights. As elsewhere, it acquired the suffix *de la frontera* ('of the frontier') during the Reconquest – probably in the 1390s – when the frontier between Moors and Christians came to rest here.

## Centro Andaluz de Flamenco

Jerez sits near the delta of the rio Guadalquivir valley, which gave Seville and Cádiz their distinctive flamenco cultures. The city's Centro Andaluz de Flamenco is a library, archive, museum and school of flamenco dedicated to keeping the tradition alive beyond the commercialised *tablaos* of the big cities. On most summer season mornings, the centre shows an hourly audio-visual presentation on the history of flamenco. *Plaza de San Juan. Open: Mon–Fri 9am–2pm (April–Oct). Free.*

## The Old Quarter

Numerous monuments jostle for attention in the historic centre. The **Alcázar**, or fortress, is smaller than those in Almería, Málaga and elsewhere but well preserved and boasts a camera obscura offering half-hourly panoramic views over the city. *Alameda Vieja. Open: daily 10am–8pm.*

Visible downhill from the Alcázar is the town's **Catedral**, whose Gothic basilica was completed in the 18th century. However, the cathedral dates back to the Mudéjar period, notably the free-standing bell tower, and earlier than that to a Moorish mosque originally built on the site. *Plaza de San Salvador. Open: daily 5.30–8pm.*

The Gothic cathedral has parts dating back to before the Reconquest

### Real Escuela Andaluz de Arte Ecuestre

Jerez's annual May Feria del Caballo (horse fair) is the biggest country fair in the entire Andalucían calendar. Outside the feria, the city's famous Real Escuela Andaluz de Arte Ecuestre is Andalucía's premier school for training horses and their riders. On some mornings you can observe dressage practice and every Thursday morning in season the school also stages a full performance in which horses and riders are accompanied by classical music.

*Avenida Duque de Abrantes. Dressage practice: Mon, Wed & Fri at noon. Admission charge. Full performance: Thur at noon (Mar–Oct). Admission charge.*

### Sherry Bodegas

The Alcázar overlooks two of Jerez's most famous bodegas, Domecq and González Byass. They and the Harvey, Sandeman, Wisdom & Warter and Williams & Humbert bodegas (all within walking distance) offer tours and tastings (mostly mornings). Booking is not necessary, but advisable if you are on a tight schedule.

*González Byass, calle Manuel González. Tel: 956 35 70 16. Open: Mon, Wed & Fri 9.30am–4.30pm. Admission charge.*
*Domecq, calle San Ildenfonso. Tel: 956 15 15 00. Open: Mon–Fri 10am–noon. Admission charge.*
*Sandeman, calle Pizarro. Tel: 956 30 11 00. Open: Mon–Fri 10am–2pm & 5–7pm. Admission charge.*
*Williams & Humbert, calle Nuño de Cañas. Tel: 956 32 40 51. Open: Mon–Fri 10am–2pm. Admission charge.*
*Harveys, calle Arcos. Tel: 956 15 10 30. Open: Mon–Fri 9.30am–1.30pm; 3–9pm. Sat 10am–1pm. Admission charge.*

Wine and, in particular, sherry has been produced in western Andalucía for at least 3000 years, having been introduced by Phoenician traders. Under Greek and Roman invaders, the Jerez region became a centre for sherry production and export throughout the Mediterranean. The teetotal Moors were largely indifferent to its alcoholic qualities, although their medicinal alembic, or still, would later find non-medical uses in distilleries around the globe.

British wine traders arrived in the pacified Spain following the Reconquest and set about carving up the sherry trade. The region's dry, chalky soil, temperate mix of sunshine and Atlantic weather systems and, most importantly of all, the *solera* (vintage, or tradition) production process made it perfect for producing sweet (*oloroso*) and dry (*fino*) sherries. Three towns or areas make up

the so-called 'Sherry Triangle': Sanlúcar de Barrameda, Jerez and the area around Cádiz and El Puerto de Santa Maria.

There are five main types of sherry, including the *oloroso* and *fino*. The latter, typified by brands such as Domecq's La Ina, is by far the more popular in bars and as an aperitif, usually drunk chilled from the fridge. Amontillado is a stronger form of fino, one in which the *flor* (yeast) has been allowed to develop a richer, sometimes dry, sometimes sweet, taste. Cream, most famously as bottled as Harvey's Bristol Cream, is a blend of *oloroso* and sun-dried Ximénez grapes.

Sherry production follows that of wine, with two crucial later stages. During fortification, distilled grape spirit is added, which increases alcohol content to 18 per cent for sweet and 15 per cent for dry. The sherry is stored for three months in wooden barrels

where young sherry is gradually filtered down through a succession of barrels containing older sherry. The final mix of old and young is then bottled. Other random processes – the quality of harvest, the appearance of *flor*, and the drying of grapes for Pedro Ximénez dessert sherry – also produce variations on the *oloroso/fino* process.

*Manzanilla*, produced exclusively in the handsome sea town of Sanlúcar de Barrameda on the mouth of the Guadalquivir, is considered an entirely different type of sherry. *Aficionados* insist that its light, drier taste is far superior to *fino*. *Manzanilla* is unfortified, and romantic myth claims that its special flavour comes from salty sea breezes blowing in across the vineyards. A more likely explanation would be soil, irrigation and climate. Just as in Jerez, Sanlúcar's *manzanilla* bodegas, such as La Guita, offer guided tours and tastings.

The third point of the Sherry Triangle is the area around Cádiz and neighbouring El Puerto de Santa María (a fast-developing tourist alternative to Cádiz itself, and served by a swift ferry service), which both produce *fino* from vineyards in the surrounding Guadalquivir valley.

*Fino* and *manzanilla* are the Andalucían tipple of choice for socialising. One of the best ways to sample *manzanilla* is at the huge tapas festival that takes place on Sanlúcar's central boulevard, Alzado de Ejercito, in the second week of October. The Andalucían passion for *jerez* reaches its peak during the February Carnaval and the September ferias, which are staggered at different dates through the month: townsfolk hang *copitas* (small glasses in leather holsters) around their necks and share bottles among themselves as they carouse in the streets.

Facing page: Sherry is stored for three months in wooden barrels
Above: Jerez is home to many sherry dynasties, including González Byass

# Cádiz

Said to be the oldest city in Europe, Cádiz has character, history, culture and lifestyle to give Seville a run for its money. Once notorious as a sleazy port full of rough bars and bordellos, it has tidied up its act over the decades while retaining the tang of its racier times. Isolated on a slender promontory jutting into the Atlantic, it is now notorious as a town that knows how to party – particularly its wild February Carnaval – and this in a region with rather more than its fair share of party towns.

Plaza España

The old town of Cádiz, north of the monumental Puertas de Tierra gates, is a maze of weather-worn mansions and monuments. A narrow street, variously named as it winds around the town, circles the seafront, and connects, for example, the RENFE station on Plaza Sevilla, the Bahia de Cádiz beach, the exquisite Parque Genovése topiary gardens and the modern Parador, the Playa de la Caleta and the Plaza de la Catedral. The city centre between these can be traversed in a matter of minutes.

The monumental Puertas de Tierra gates

### Catedral Nuevo

Cádiz's cathedral, called the 'new' cathedral because it sits on the site of an earlier church, is a mountainous Baroque and Neo-classical edifice looming magnificently over the Plaza de la Catedral. Its bright yellow-orange tiled cupola and Neo-classical towers act as a guidance beacon wherever you walk across town. Although of minor historic detail, it is noted as the last resting place of probably the most famous *gaditano*, as the people of Cádiz are known, composer Manuel de Falla (1876–1946). *Plaza de la Catedral. Open: Mon–Sat 10am–1pm & 5.30–7pm. Admission charge.*

### La Vida Gaditano

As well as its historic Carnaval, Cádiz has a very lively university culture supporting music venues, clubs, book and music stores, and a high profile gay community who are the life and soul of Carnaval and just about any other excuse to party. It also goes without saying that Cádiz is a fish-eater's paradise: only a fool would leave Cádiz without sampling either the restaurant or tapas bar at its legendary El Faro (*calle San Felix 15*).

## Museo de Bellas Artes

Near the cathedral, the museum dedicated to the history and culture of Cádiz tracks the city's development from prehistoric times to the present day. On its second floor is a sizeable art gallery, dedicated to works by Murillo, Rubens and Zurburán.
*Plaza de Mina. Open: Tue–Sat 9.30am–8pm, Sun 9.30am–2pm. Free.*

The Catedral Nuevo from the seafront

## Museo Histórico Municipal

The history of this famously liberal city is celebrated in the city museum, which displays many of the papers relating to the short-lived independent government of the 1810s. Its neighbouring **Oratorio de San Felipe Neri** is the place where the Cortes sat and is also open to the public.
*Calle Sante Inés. Museo open: Tue–Fri 9am–1pm & 4–7pm. Sat–Sun 9am–1pm. Free.*
*Oratorio open: Mon–Sat 10am–1.30pm. Admission charge.*

## Plaza España

Much of historic Cádiz is centred around the Plaza España, which is dominated by the **Monumento a las Cortes Liberales,** the monument to Spain's first liberal government, established briefly in Cádiz in the 1810s before being quashed by the monarchy.

## Torre Tavira

This 18th-century watchtower in the heights above the city is just one of the numerous military installations that offer spectacular views back over Cádiz. It features a camera obscura with a 360-degree panorama of the city.
*Calle Marqués de Real Tesoro. Open: daily 10am–6pm.*

# Walk: Cádiz

Cádiz is the perfect walking city, a maze of 18th-century streets and squares crammed into the tip of a slender promontory jutting into the Atlantic. With most new-build projects – the motel-like Atlantico *parador* excepted – barred from the old town, it is also the most atmospheric of all the *cascos antiguos* (old towns) of Andalucía.
*Allow 3 hours.*

## 1 Puertas de Tierra

These monumental walls were part of the city's 18th-century defences when Andalucía's world trade centre moved to Cádiz from Seville following the silting of the rio Guadalquivir.

## 2 Carcel Vieja

This walk heads west into the morning sun along Concepción Arenal and past the Carcel Vieja, or old prison, towards the cathedral.

Playa de la Caleta, Cádiz's most popular beach

## 3 Catedral Nuevo

The cathedral looms over the Plaza de Pio XII (Pope Pius 12th), also known as the Plaza de la Catedral. Cathedral and square give off a weird oceanic light like a glow from the sea just behind it.
*Follow the sea road on towards the Castillo de San Sebastian fortifications (not open to the public).*

## 4 Playa de la Caleta

The fortifications overlook one of Cádiz's most popular beaches, the Playa de la Caleta. *Continue along the sea road to the Castillo de Santa Catalina.*

## 5 Castillo de Santa Catalina

At the north end of the bay, matching the Sebastian sea defences across the bay, sits the star-shaped citadel of Santa Catalina, built in 1598.
*Open: Mon–Fri 10am–6pm, Sat–Sun 10am–1pm. Free.*

## 6 Parque del Genovése

From the Castillo, these exquisitely sculpted topiary walkways look like a

backdrop out of a de Chirico painting.
*Turn right at the southern end of the park
along calle Benito Perez Galdos.*

### 7 Calle Benito Perez Galdos

The calle heads into the heart of the
town to the Gran Teatro Falla and its
plaza. Continue straight on to the
Oratorio de San Felipe Neri and the
Museo Histórico Municipal, site of and
archive to the historic 1812 constitution.
*From here you can either retrace your
steps to follow the sea road or head a few
blocks north via calle Sagasta to the
Plazas de San Francisco and de Mina.*

### 8 Museo de Bellas Artes y Arqueológico

The Museo de Bellas Artes y

Arqueológico has Phoenician and
Roman displays on its ground floor, a
fine arts collection including works by
Rubens, Zurburán and Murillo on the
second and an ethnology department.
*Open: Tue 2.30–8pm, Wed–Sat
9am–8pm, Sun 9.30am–2pm. Admission
charge (EU citizens free).*

### 9 Plaza de España

A few blocks east of Plaza del Mina is the
Plaza de España. Beyond it lies the
seafront of the Puerto Commercial;
northwards, steps lead up on to modern-
day defences with views back down over
the town.
*The Avenida del Puerto runs eastwards to
the Paseo de Canalejas and the Plaza de
San Juan de Dios.*

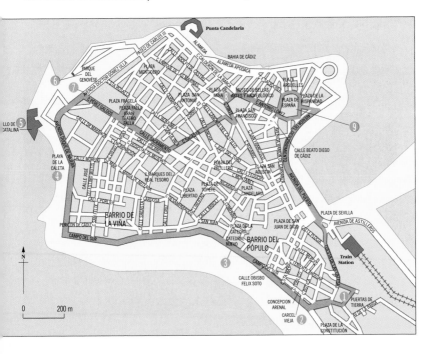

Wherever you go in Andalucía in the week running up to Lent, you will find communities large and small celebrating Carnaval, although none of them with the hair-raising vigour of Cádiz. Like the pre-Christian saturnalias that prefigured it, Carnaval is the last chance to unwind before the forty days of austerity.

Community and religious groups, professional and youth organisations, and groups of friends roam the streets (usually in the evening and late at night) entertaining crowds, bars and restaurants with pithy and sometimes rude or libellous satires on events of the day. Most groups will enter competitions judged in the town theatre, such as Cádiz's Teatro Falla, while others just take to the streets for the hell of it. Others, such as Cádiz's party-prone gay community, seize the opportunity to run amok in drag, fancy dress, or as *gigantes*, blobby monsters wielding balloons on sticks on a mission to hunt down every child and tourist and wallop them over the head.

The idea, as perhaps is already apparent, is to have as much good-natured fun as is possible this side of getting arrested. And compared to similar events elsewhere in Europe, Andalucía's Carnavales are remarkably good-natured and convivial affairs. Each climaxes in a *cabalgata*, or cavalcade, where, however modest the display, children of every conceivable age find themselves engulfed in blizzards of

confetti and confectionery hurled by retinues of the town's beauty queens from their gaudily decorated floats.

The notoriety of Cádiz's Carnaval, which stems from both its rumbustious seaport culture and its healthy tradition of resistance to state control, is given further resonance by the fact that it was the only Carnaval that Franco was too scared to ban, fearing that a ban might spark insurrection. It is very much a celebration in the hands of the people, and one where the revellers in this most poverty-stricken region of Spain have over the centuries found at least symbolic ways to wreak revenge on bosses, politicians and the hated *caciques* (foremen) of the despised *latifundistas*.

Even on the storm-prone Atlantic coast, February can be kind and sunny during daytimes, although evenings can be distinctly chilly. Most revellers seem to survive on piping hot food, alcohol, aerobic motion among the crowds in the streets and generously layered undergarments.

Anyone hoping to join the celebrations in Cádiz itself, and to a lesser degree in Seville and Granada, should begin planning and making accommodation enquiries the preceding autumn – Cádiz's hotels can fill up months ahead for Carnaval. Alternatives include staying in the burgeoning resort of Puerto de Santa María across the Bahía de Cádiz, with ferry connections to Cádiz's old town during daytimes, or further afield in Jerez or Seville. Late night and early morning trains to both are often full of revellers returning home from Cádiz, and both cities will also be celebrating their own Carnavales. Any of the larger cities will provide a launchpad to smaller, local Carnavales, with tourist offices able to supply key days and venues, and which, while modest, offer a glimpse into *la vida Andaluz* unseen by the summer visitor.

Andalucía's Carnavales are good-natured and convivial affairs

# Costa de la Luz

Spain's little-visited Atlantic Costa de la Luz – coast of light – is one of the best-kept secrets in Europe. Although the great rio Guadalquivir estuary and a number of ports interrupt it, its 200km (150-mile) beach is the longest – and cleanest – in Spain, perhaps the whole of southern Europe. Its climate is also kinder than you might expect from an Atlantic coastline.

Tarifa beach

Stretching from medieval Tarifa (*see pp72–3*) to Isla Cristina near the Portuguese border, the costa passes two of Spain's greatest sea ports, the largest bird and nature reserve in Europe, Roman ruins, various grand seaside towns and the most unspoilt beaches in the whole of Spain. It also had a key role when Seville was the front office for a colonial enterprise stretching halfway around the globe.

### History

As the handsome Roman ruins of Bolonia (*see pp70–1*) north of Tarifa's world-class surf beaches (*see pp72–3*) attest, explorers had rounded the Pillars of Hercules to explore Atlantic Spain as early as the second century BC. Bolonia became famous throughout the Empire for a spicy fish paste, garum, used as a relish by the wealthier classes.

Even earlier settlers such as the Phoenicians had already brought viniculture to the region, at Cádiz and elsewhere, and fishing ports at Zahara de los Atunes and its (rather scruffy) neighbour, Barbate. The latter does, however, have one major claim to fame:

nearby Cabo de Trafalgar overlooked the 1805 battle which saw England's fleet under Nelson defeat the French and Spanish, although at some personal cost to the admiral.

### Resorts

The main reason that the Costa de la Luz is one of Europe's best-kept secrets is that holidaymakers from Seville, Cádiz, Huelva and elsewhere tend to keep resorts such as **Conil** and **Chiclana** to themselves. Both are classic bucket-and-spade resorts, with little else to commend them, although Conil has a photogenic town square and medieval tower with connections to the legend of Guzman the Good, defender of Tarifa (*see pp72–3*).

The coast of light vanishes beneath the salty lagoons of Cádiz to re-emerge at the garish resort of **Rota**, a favourite for US servicefolk on R&R, and the golden strands of **Chipiona**. However, given the proximity of **Sanlúcar de Barrameda**, the traveller should push on to this extremely atmospheric town with its mansions, *manzanilla* bodegas and fine beaches.

Drivers and pedestrians alike will find themselves driven inland by the twin natural barriers of the rio Guadalquivir and the 200,000 acre wetland nature reserve, the **Parque Nacional de Doñana** (*see pp66–7*). The costa resumes at the busy resort of **Matalascañas** (the northern entrance to the national park), and continues along fine deserted beaches and dunes to the low-key seaside town of **Mazagon**.

The noisy industrial city of **Huelva** is largely missable, although a useful base if you want to explore the various Columbus sites nearby (*see pp64–5*). Completists, loners and golfers might, however, want to explore Huelva's nearest resort, **Punta Umbria**, and **Isla Cristina** itself – in fact an isthmus with a working fishing port at its heart – and **Cristallina**, a golf/convention-centre and hotel complex some 10km (6.25m) away down those unspoilt dunes. Head for the former for authentic atmosphere, the latter for creature comforts.

One of the best beaches on the entire Costa de la Luz, below Valdevaqueros dune system

History may have changed its attitude towards 15th-century explorer Christopher Columbus recently, but he remains very much a hero in western Andalucía. He sailed from Palos de la Frontera (near Huelva), Seville, Cádiz and Sanlúcar de Barrameda on his four voyages to the Americas, and is celebrated in statuary and other monuments throughout the region.

Born in Genoa, Italy, in 1451, Cristóbal Colón, as he is more commonly known in Spain, gained his reputation as an adventurer in the Mediterranean and Iberian Atlantic before deciding to search for the fabled westerly route to the Orient. Portugal rebuffed his proposal, but the Spanish monarchs Isabel and Fernando (the former especially) agreed to fund his expedition.

Colón returned from one of his four expeditions to the Americas a criminal in chains, following his disastrous mismanagement of an uprising, and his treatment of indigenous Americans was appalling, if par for the era. Yet his piracy and plunder funded Spain's Golden Age, and sketched out a map of geopolitics still discernible today.

## La Rábida

This monastery at the mouth of the rio Tinto estuary south of Huelva is the main Colón site in Andalucía. He visited the monastery while pursuing support for his expedition, debating with its theologians and seeking divine guidance for his schemes. Today, the monastery is part of a larger theme-park-like enclosure, with gardens, exhibits, and replicas of the caravelles *Santa María*,

*Nina* and *Pinta* with which he sailed on his first voyage in 1492.

Guided tours of the monastery run almost hourly each day, taking in his living quarters, murals of the expeditions and the chapel where fellow explorer Martín Alonso Pinzón, captain of the *Pinta*, is interred.

The replicas of Colón's three ships are moored at the **Muelle de las Carabellas** (caravel pier), where there is also an exhibit dedicated to his life and exploits.

*Monasterio de La Rábida: 8km S of Huelva on N-442. Tel: 959 35 04 11. Open: Tue–Sun 10am–1pm & 4–6pm (hourly tours). Closed: Mon. Free, but donations welcome. Muelle de las Carabellas open: Tue–Fri 10am–2pm, Sat–Sun 11am–8pm. Closed: Mon. Admission charge.*

## Palos de la Frontera

This small village a short journey inland from Rábida is the port from which Colón and his crew left in 1492. The captains of the *Pinta* and *Nina*, cousins Martín and Vicénte Yañez Pinzón, came from here, and they and their crews are celebrated in a monument outside the beautiful town **church**, where Colón and his men celebrated communion on the eve of departure, and in the **Museo Martín Alonso Pinzón** in the town centre.

*Museo Martín Alonso Pinzón, calle Cristóbal Colón 24. Open: Tue–Sun 10am–1pm & 5–7pm. Closed: Mon. Free.*

### Moguer

This immensely atmospheric, if slightly crumbly, town further inland on the rio Tinto is where many of the three ships' crews came from. The most noteworthy connection with the Colón legend is the **Convento Santa Clara**, where Colón honoured a promise, made when he was spared a storm that nearly wrecked the enterprise off the Azores, to keep a vigil for a night on his return from the 1492 voyage.

*Convento Santa Clara, calle Monjas. Open: guided visits Tue–Sat 11am–noon & 5–7pm. Closed: Mon & holidays. Free.*

Facing page: Replica boats at La Rábida, near Huelva
Above: The Columbus statue at La Rábida

# Coto Doñana

The largest nature reserve in Spain and one of the largest in Europe, the Coto Doñana stretches from Sanlúcar's further shore halfway to Seville, north as far as El Rocio and halfway up to Huelva along the Costa de la Luz (*see pp62–3*). As well as its indigenous wildlife, it is also a stopping-off point for an estimated six million migratory birds on their biennial routes north and south in spring and autumn.

Parkland walkway

### Terrain

The Parque Nacional de Doñana was declared a protected area in 1969 for fear that encroaching farming and development might threaten this unique wetland environment. Scientists in fact describe the region as man-made, as over the centuries farming, fishing, hunting and other activities have subtly and not-so-subtly altered its shape and the biota it supports. The park comprises the *marismas* (marshes) of the rios Guadalquivir and Guadiamar, the former here debouching into the Atlantic after its journey from its source 700km (435 miles) away in the Sierra de Cazorla in northwest Andalucía.

The need to protect the wetlands was made dramatically apparent in 1988 when a reservoir at a mine north of the park, holding millions of cubic metres of toxic sludge, burst its banks and flooded the rio Guadiamar. Barriers hastily erected by embarrassed authorities prevented all but a small part of the Doñana being polluted, but even after an extensive clean-up there are fears that heavy metals and other toxins may have entered the food chain. Politicians are still debating how to complete the clean-up, and perhaps unsurprisingly the mine that caused the disaster is still in action.

### Wildlife

As well as its migratory visitors, which in winter months include vast flocks of flamingos feasting on shrimp, the park is also home to fallow and red deer, lynx, boar, mongoose and several rare raptors, including the imperial eagle.

### Access

Human visitors, however, are limited to a few hundred daily, and those only by organised four-wheel guided tour, booked (well) in advance, from visitor centres on either side of the Guadalquivir. The 28km (17.4 miles) of beach from the resort of Matalascañas south to the tip of the park are accessible to walkers, but inland is off-limits and, in fact, largely inaccessible without special craft.

The commonest route of entry into the park is via the **Centro de Visitantes**

Only a few hundred visitors a day are allowed into the 200,000 acre nature reserve

**El Acebuche**, in the small village of Acebuche inland from Matalascañas. This organises morning and afternoon four-hour 'safaris' in four-wheel vehicles. An alternative is a guided tour organised from Sanlúcar by a commercial agency such as **Viajes Doñana**. Boat trips along the Guadalquivir, either from Sanlúcar or Seville, often include a short walking tour of a smaller area of the park. None of these can promise a glimpse of the rarer creatures lurking in the park – serious birders should enquire at the Acebuche centre about hides, particularly at the **Centro de Visitantes José Antonio Valverde** at the northern edge of the park. The park itself is a spookily beautiful human-free wilderness. If it is an important part of your itinerary, enquire well in advance; you may even want to build a tour around it.

*Centro de Visitantes El Acebuche, Acebuche. Tel: 959 43 04 32. Admission charge for tours.*

*Viajes Doñana, Sanlúcar de Barrameda. Tel: 956 36 25 40. Admission charge for tours.*

what to see

Iglesia del Divino Salvador, Vejer

# Arcos to Vejer de la Frontera

This gaggle of strays – Arcos de la Frontera, Medina Sedonia and Vejer de la Frontera – from the main, easterly, swarm of the Pueblos Blancos, Andalucía's famous white villages (*see pp80–1*), is best visited from the western edges of Andalucía. Conveniently, the three towns also offer a swift alternative route between Seville and the Costa de la Luz (*see pp62–3*) as well as connections in both easterly and westerly directions.

### Arcos de la Frontera

Arcos is the most impressive of the Pueblos Blancos after Ronda. It too sits on its own defensive bluff, 100m (328ft) above the rio Guadalete and something of a geological anomaly in the surroundings of gentle rolling farmland, in this southerly part of Seville's 'frying pan'.

Vejer's magnificent Plaza de Espāna fountain

Arcos's compact *casco antiguo* (old town) is barely a two-minute sprint across in any direction, but its narrow streets and alleys bulge with marvels over a thousand years old. The **Castillo de los Duques**, after the family that owned Arcos for centuries, dates back to the 11th century, although its interior is closed to the public. The 15th-century **Iglesia de San Pedro** bell-tower has a deafening triple carillon that stops people in their tracks on the hour. The **Convento de la Encarnación** and the **Palacio del Conde de Águila** are among the oldest façades, and the tourist office, in the square opposite the *parador*, has guides to all of Arcos's monuments. *Iglesia de San Pedro, calle Núñez de Prado. Open: Mon–Fri 10am–1pm & 4–6pm, Sat 10am–2pm. Closed: Sun. Admission charge.*

### Medina Sidonia

Medina Sidonia, another hilltop redoubt, is famed as the seat awarded to the family of Guzman el Bueno (the Good), defender of Tarifa (*see pp70–1*).

The Duques de Medina Sidonia continue to oversee the town: the latest incumbent is the firebrand socialist Duchess of Medina Sidonia.

The town's central Plaza España is home to both an impressive 17th-century *ayuntamiento* (town council) building and Medina's star attraction, the **Iglesia Santa María la Coronada**, which contains some remarkable votary art and details dating back to the period in the 16th century when it also served as local headquarters for the Inquisition. The ruins of Roman sewers, still visible on the outskirts of town suggest that Medina was an important settlement in pre-Christian times, and its three monumental Moorish gates suggest that it also held similar office prior to the Reconquest.

*Iglesia Santa María Coronada, Plaza España. Open: daily 10.30am–2pm & 5.30–9pm.*
*Admission charge.*

### Vejer de la Frontera

It has at least two other rivals for the title, but Vejer has to be one of, if not the, most exquisite and archetypal of the Pueblos Blancos: a tangle of whitewashed streets and alleys atop a defensive bluff with panoramic views and many of its defences still intact.

Although it has an impressive 16th-century church, the **Iglesia del Divino Salvador**, and parts of the **castle** are also open to the public, the best way to see Vejer is simply to wander its alleys, ramparts and squares, many of them with fantastic views down over the Costa de la Luz. The **Plaza de España**, with an outrageous Triana-tiled fountain and the smart new El Caliph hotel, is the place to head for lunch or a drink.

*Iglesia del Divino Salvador, calle Ramón y Cajal. Open: daily 11am–1pm & 7–9pm.*
*Admission charge.*
*Castillo open: daily 11am–2pm & 5–9pm.*
*Free.*

Arcos de la Frontera resplendent on its bluff over the rio Guadalete

Andalucía occupied a position of great privilege in the western Roman Empire for 500 years from the 2nd century BC to the 3rd century AD. Following centuries of brutal rule by Carthage, the great Mediterranean force in what is nowadays Tunisia, the inhabitants of the southwestern tip of the peninsula welcomed the Roman invaders, and certainly thrived on the culture they introduced. Roman Baetica, as the region was known, was almost identical in outline to modern-day Andalucía.

Carthage was already on the wane when the Romans invaded this part of the peninsula in the last decade of the 3rd century BC. They began construction of their greatest settlement, Italica, just north of Seville, in 206 BC. The thriving seaport at modern-day Bolonia, Baelo Claudia (named after the emperor Claudius) followed. So, in the 1st century

AD, did Acinipo, the extensive ruined settlement on a windswept bluff outside Ronda, known to centuries of pilfering landscape gardeners (the Brits worst of all) as Ronda la Vieja, 'old Ronda'.

## Italica

At its height, around the 1st century AD, Italica was one of the greatest cities in the Roman Empire, a rival to even Alexandria and Rome. Its population reached half a million, and its monumental amphitheatre, visible in part today, held in excess of 25,000 people. The Visigoths simply abandoned the site for their preferred base of Seville, while later rulers plundered the site for materials (including the stone columns that now surround Seville Cathedral).

Also still visible are the vestiges of several halls and mosaics, foundations and men's and women's baths.

*Italica, Santiponce. 5km (3 miles) north of Seville on E-803. Open: Tue–Sat 9am–8pm, Sun 10am–3pm (Apr–Sept); Tue–Sat 9am–5.30pm, Sun 10am–4pm (Oct–Mar). Admission charge (EU citizens free).*

## Baelo Claudia

This smaller but less vandalised site sits on the beach at Bolonia north of Tarifa. Although less impressive than Italica it includes the remains of a forum, baths, an open-air auditorium, temples to Juno, Jupiter and Minerva, and other religious buildings. Near the beach is the vestigial fish factory responsible for garum, an alarming paste of fish parts that was shipped throughout the empire and revered as the best caviar is today.

Like Acinipo (*see below*) Baelo Claudia is an archaeological site still under excavation, and much more is expected to be revealed on the perimeter of the current site.

*Baelo Claudia, Bolonia beach. 15km (9 miles) north of Tarifa on N-340. Open: daily 10am–2.30pm & 4–5.30pm. Admission charge.*

## Acinipo/Ronda la Vieja

Known by either of these names on local maps and road signs, this has one of the most spectacular settings in the whole of Andalucía: it lies on a dip slope rising to one of a series of bluffs above rolling farmland east of Ronda, with views of the sierras to the north.

A dig in progress like Baelo Claudia, Acinipo has so far yielded a magnificent open-air theatre and auditorium, the groundworks of a triple hot water baths, fragments of a forum, a skeletal street grid and piles of what were once the rock walls of the town itself. Its remote site left it prone to ransackers over the centuries, and parts have actually turned up in nearby domestic gardens (where nervous museum curators have left them in comparative safety). Bits of Acinipo are still being stolen into the 21st century.

*Acinipo, on MA-499 Ronda–Setenil. Open: Tue–Sat 11am–5pm, Sun 11am–3pm. Free.*

Facing page above: The windswept Roman ruins of Ronda la Vieja, 'old Ronda'
Facing page below: Vestigial remains at Bolonia
Below: Backstage at the monumental theatre in Roman Acinipo

# Tarifa and the Surf Coast

In recent years Tarifa has been declared the most fashionable medieval city in Spain, possibly one of the most fashionable in the whole of Europe. An accident of local winds and tides, an embarrassment of glorious sandy beaches and the efforts of the surfie grapevine have elected it one of the three great surf destinations in the world.

Tarifa's Mudéjar Puerta de Jerez

The town is named after its 8th-century invader, Tarif ben Maluk, who made a successful sortie to the European mainland to scout the land for Tariq ibn Ziyad's invasion of Gibraltar in AD 711. While its medieval walls and street plan remain, it has changed rather drastically over the past decade. Every other storefront in its maze-like walled Moorish old town is a boutique, gear store, cybercafé or bar dedicated to the shrimpcatcher-shorts set. Traditionally a laid-back hideaway, popular with backpackers on their way to and from north Africa, its new-age emporia now find themselves serving a new generation of beach bums.

Tarifa is also, unsurprisingly, a party town, nowhere more so than in the bars, cafés and restaurants around calle Sancho IV in the centre. It is also worth pointing out that while some of its best hotels, such as the Amarillo and la Sacristia, are here, most visitors head for the beach hotels such as the Hurricane and Dos Mares a dozen or so kilometres north.

Tarifa's beaches themselves begin unprepossessingly but improve around the Hurricane hotel and are at their best by the dune systems of Valdevaqueros, where hardcore surfers can be found at play year-round.

## Castillo de Guzmán

Parts of the handsome ramparts are still used by the Spanish naval authorities and off-limits to visitors, but Tarifa's most imposing structure, the Castillo de Guzmán, has recently been restored and reopened to the public. Built on the site of a 10th-century Moorish alcázar, itself built on the site of a Roman fort, this was rebuilt as a *Reconquista* castle in the 11th century. The castle acquired its name and its place in history during the 1292 Moorish siege of Tarifa, when the Christians defended the town against invaders from Morocco. Its name derives from the honorific title awarded by the people to Alonso Pérez Guzmán, Guzmán el Bueno (Guzmán the Good), the castle's commander, who sacrificed his son, who had been taken hostage by the invaders rather than surrender the town. *Calle Guzmán. Open: daily 10am–2pm & 6–8pm. Admission charge.*

## Iglesia de San Mateo

Also of interest is the Iglesia de San Mateo, on the corner of calles Moscardo

and Copons, begun in the 15th century but only completed in the 18th. The dilapidated Baroque exterior conceals a surprisingly modern interior.
*Open: daily 9am–1pm & 6.30–8pm. Free.*

## Museo Municipal

Near the castle, on the picturesque Plaza de Santa María, are the *ayuntamiento* and the small Museo Municipal, with a modest but respectable collection of neolithic, Roman and Moorish artefacts.
*Museo Municipal, Plaza de Santa María. Open: daily 11am–1pm. Free.*

## Whale Watching

As well as surfie boutiques, Tarifa has more than its fair share of emporia offering dolphin- and whale-watching expeditions. The most ecologically sound thing to do would be to leave these beautiful creatures in peace, but if you have to see them it's best to go with non-profit-making organisations such as Whale Watch (*Paseo de la Alameda; tel: 956 68 47 76*) or the Foundation for Information and Research on Marine Mammals (*calle Pedro Cortés; tel: 956 62 70 08*).

Kite surfing, mixing parachuting with windsurfing, at Tarifa beach

Gibraltar's Rock

# Gibraltar

As the disputed landmass at the western tip of Andalucía grinds towards some sort of resolution of the sovereignty issue, it seems likely that few Gibraltarians will be happy with the outcome. Depending on who you listen to, its 30,000 inhabitants are either all blue-blooded patriotic Brits, or a culturally diverse mix of Africans, Spaniards, Jews, Maltese and Genoese who are happy with the status quo and distrustful of their garrulous larger neighbour.

A stroll along Gibraltar's central Main Street, with its preponderance of duty-free stores, fast food outlets and British pubs, might have you assuming that this is truly a British enclave. Old Gibraltar hands, however, point out that there is another Gibraltar away from this shopping mall-cum-virtual casino, in its handsome old back streets and squares.

Main Street, Gibraltar's liveliest thoroughfare

## Information
**Passports and Visas**
As the odd disappointed shopper or baffled taxi driver discovers, you need a passport to pass between Spain and Gibraltar. Visitors from EU countries, the USA, Canada, Israel and South Africa do not require visas: visitors from elsewhere should check the current state of visa requirements before visiting what is still a sensitive military base – Gibraltar still has an active British military presence.

**Getting There and Around**
Drivers are advised to park in Spain and walk across the border: delays are frequent and access is cut off whenever a flight lands on the runway of the small but busy airport between the border and the centre.

Visitors on foot will find various agencies touting for day and half-day tours on the Gibraltar side of the border, and travel agencies in the centre also offer tours of the Rock, much of which can be visited on foot or by bus and cable car. For non-drivers, there are local and regional bus connections with La Linea de la Concepción, the town on the Spanish side of the border crossing, and bus or taxi links between the rail stations at either San Roque/La Linea or Algeciras.

The Tourism Office on Cathedral Square can also advise on options for visiting the Rock itself: two- to four-hour minibus tours are available, and it's also feasible to write your own itinerary using buses or cabs. In fact, most routes on the Rock itself are self-guiding and depend on how much time you have.
*Tourism Office, Cathedral Square. Tel: 74950 (local only: prefix 956 from Spain) for tours.*

There are a number of excellent hotels on 'the Rock', not least the redoubtable and recently renovated The Rock hotel, although most visitors might find a day sufficient to cover most bases.

If you are approaching Gibraltar on a day trip, check the weather beforehand: the Rock can be a magnet for bad weather, which wreaths it in cloud and closes the cable car. A word of warning: be wary around the 'apes', which are in fact macaque monkeys, on the Rock: they have been known to snatch bags or cameras for sport, and can be aggressive if approached.

**Money**
Gibraltar trades in Gibraltarian sterling, not negotiable elsewhere, or the euro.

Cute but dangerous: the Rock's macaque monkeys are notorious bag snatchers and can bite

## What to See
### Casemates Square
This should be the first port of call: the scene of most public celebrations, it is also home to some of Gibraltar's favourite restaurants, such as Nelson's.

### Gibraltar Museum
Halfway along Main Street, to the right beyond the Cathedral of St Mary the Crowned, is the Gibraltar Museum. Its small but impressive display of artefacts ranges from the Moorish invasion of the Iberian peninsula up to its maritime exploits in recent centuries.
*Gibraltar Museum, Bomb House Lane. Open: Mon–Fri 10am–6pm, Sat 10am–2pm. Admission charge.*

# Ronda and the Pueblos Blancos

Coincidences of geography, landscape, climate and history have made the town of Ronda and its surrounding Pueblos Blancos, the white villages of Andalucía, a honeypot attraction for visitors. Ronda, which overtook Córdoba in 2002 as the third most-visited destination in Andalucía, sits equidistant between Seville, Granada, Málaga and Gibraltar, and has good road and rail connections with all four cities.

Ronda's Puente Nuevo bridge

The distribution of its smaller siblings, all within an hour by bus or car from Ronda on its bluff in the Serrania de Ronda mountains, makes it a perfect base for exploring, and the pueblos have become one of the key destinations in the region.

Tourism has been changing in Ronda in recent years, with new independent hotels opening in and around the town and new restaurants, nightclubs and bars opening to cater to independent travellers who stay longer than the traditional day trippers from the Costa del Sol resorts.

As a stroll around its old town, across the 100m (273ft) high Puente Nuevo ('new bridge'), over the Tajo gorge and rio Guadalevin will show, Ronda's history stretches back to the Roman era and even earlier.

### Plaza de Toros

Famously, Ronda is the birthplace of 'modern', that is, on foot, bullfighting, pioneered by legendary matador Pedro Romero in the town's Plaza de Toros

(bullring) in the 18th century. Unfortunately, today the Plaza is largely a museum, used only once a year in early September for the annual Goyesca *corrida*, or bullfight, that climaxes the September *feria* or fair. Tickets for the Goyesca, in which matadors, picadors and other participants dress in the manner of Goya's paintings of the bullfight (*see pp78–9*), often sell out in advance, and can cost as much as €80 (£50) each in the *sombra* (shade).
*Plaza de Toros. Museum open: daily 10am–7pm. Admission charge.*

### La Ciudad (Old Town)

An anticlockwise route around the old town, taking the first right-hand turning over the bridge, will lead to Ronda's most impressive monument, the **Palacio de Mondragon**, a renovated Moorish palace now used as town museum, a language school and conference centre. Its beautiful miniature water gardens teeter on the battlements that surround the old town.
*Open: Mon–Fri 10am–6pm, Sat–Sun*

10am–3pm. Admission charge (EU citizens free).

Beyond the Mondragon is the handsome **Plaza de Duques de Parcent**, with the unusual arcaded *ayuntamiento* and neighbouring **Santa María la Mayor** church with its Trumpton-Baroque belltower (*open: daily 10am–7pm; admission charge*).

Downhill from the Plaza, calle Armiñan leads to the monumental **Iglesia del Espiritu Santo** (*open: daily 10am–6pm; admission charge*), the dramatic Moorish gates and, next to the church, Ronda's trendy arts café/gallery/venue, Enfrente Arte. Calle Marques de Salvatierra, off Calle Armiñan, leads down to the **Baños Árabes** (Arab baths) (*open: Tue 3–5.30pm, Wed–Sat 10am–2pm &*

3–5.30pm, Sun 10am–2pm; free*), below the Moorish and Roman bridges that spanned the river before the Puente Nuevo was built in the 18th century.

The new road beyond the baths circles below the town battlements, which are accessible via a path rising above the baths. Alternatively, steps lead up from the traditional working class *barrio* of Ocho Caños ('eight pipes', the fountain by the church here) to the centre of the Mercadillo, or new town, district.

Ronda's most breathtaking views are the public walkway behind the *parador* (next to the Puente Nuevo) and further along in the leafy Alameda. Special mention must be made of the stunning but very friendly Michelin-starred Tragabuches restaurant, just to the right of the *parador*.

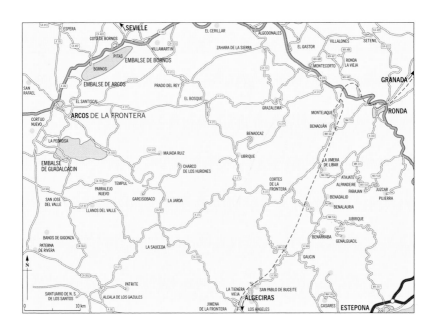

## The Corrida

Bullfighting probably originated as a gladiatorial sport, pitting man, mounted or on foot, against a single bull, in Roman or Moorish times. It acquired its layers of robing and ritual – the *traje de luz* (suit of lights), that every matador wears, the *picadores* and *banderilleros* who assist the matador – over the centuries. It was codified in places such as the great equestrian centre Jerez and, later, Ronda, in the 18th century, where legendary matador Pedro Romero 'invented' modern, on foot, bullfighting.

The *corrida* has its rhythms, which are measured out by the *presidente*, the president of the fight or bullring, and accompanying brass band: it is up to the *presidente* to judge the progress of the *corrida*, and to usher the action on through its three key stages. In the case of a particularly disastrous performance by either matador or bull, he can also dismiss either or both from the ring, to the shame of the former, and the crowd can actually petition for a brave bull to be freed, usually by waving white handkerchiefs.

The first stage of the *corrida*, the *tercio de varas*, is the initial engagement between matador and bull, where the former may leave the bull to the goading of his *peones*, unmounted assistants who taunt the bull with capes. They are joined by *picadores*, mounted on padded horses, who engage the bull by plunging long lances into its spine, weakening its back and neck muscles. It is quite common for their heavily padded and blindfolded horses to be flipped by the enraged bull.

In the *tercio de banderillas*, unmounted assistants, *bandilleros*, often in *trajes de luces* themselves, feint at the bull and plunge *bandilleras* (long beribboned darts) into its back, further weakening the animal.

The final stage – if all goes to plan – is the *estocada*, or death blow, where the matador will judge the bull's strength by various passes of the *muleta*, the famed red cape. The perfect *estocada*, rarely seen, is the *estocada recibiendo*, in which the matador allows the bull to charge, meets it and deals a death blow to the spinal column with his sword. Sometimes, however, especially with younger matadors fighting *novilladas*, the *estocada* is not struck, and it is not uncommon for *peones* to have to finish the bull off with a bolt-gun to the forehead before it is dragged from the plaza de toros.

The *corrida* has been controversial ever since non-Spanish visitors arrived en masse. Under 50 per cent of Spaniards are said to follow the *corrida*, but those who do pursue it with the sort of passion that the English reserve for cup final football. Matadors, especially local heroes, are treated like pop stars, and even bulls are cheered during especially good bullfights. An estimated 25,000 bulls are killed in *corridas* across Spain

each year, a fraction of the cattle culled in recent health scares across Europe. Until its day in the plaza de toros, the *toro bravo* (fighting bull) has led a pampered bachelor life in the fields of the *ganaderia*, the large ranches common in southwestern Andalucía.

The corrida, bullfight, invented in Andalucía, modernised in Ronda

# Pueblos Blancos

Visiting the Pueblos Blancos, from Seville, Ronda or the Costa del Sol, depends on two things: time and transport. With a car the main pueblos could be seen in a couple of days, although the driver would be missing some of the finest landscapes in Andalucía. With time, using public transport and the odd taxi is an ideal way to tour the villages. It's even possible to tour them by cycle or on foot.

Gaucin and its castle

### Grazalema

The most famous pueblo, Grazalema sits high on a peak and is said to be the rainiest town in Spain. Its pretty town square is busy most afternoons all year round, and on Mondays a market materialises in the town car park nearby. Cadiz el Chico on the square is the place for local speciality dishes using wild thistles (think tree-sized greens) and there are now four hotels here, two of which (La Puerta and the Fuente) are four-star.

### Zahara de las Sierras

A car is necessary to reach the breathtaking Puerta de las Palomas ('Pass of the Doves') above Grazalema. From here you can look down on little-visited Zahara de las Sierras, on its windswept peak overlooking a vast *embalse*, or reservoir. The obligatory ruined Moorish castle at the top of Zahara's craggy pinnacle is the best preserved in the region, with 360 degree views. There are two hotels here, the central Marqués de Zahara, and the Arcos de la Villa, with views across the valley.

### Setenil de las Bodegas

A roundabout but extremely picturesque route from Zahara leads across country to one of the strangest of all the Pueblos Blancos: Setenil de las Bodegas. The road below Zahara continues around the embalse, on to the Seville–Ronda road and off it again just before Ronda, heading for Roman Acinipo (*see pp70–1*). Beyond Acinipo, through glorious rolling farmland, lies the sunken cave village of Setenil.

Where the great majority of Pueblos Blancos were built on inaccessible bluffs for defensive reasons before and during the Moorish presence and the Reconquest, Setenil was built over caves hidden in the valley of the rio Trejo, first inhabited in pre-Christian times. Today, its houses seem to emerge from the rock, and many have olive groves on their roofs. The presence of only one hotel, El Almendral, testifies to Setenil's position off the beaten track.

### Olvera

North of Setenil, Olvera is interesting for its church, and its reputation as one of the worst 19th-century bandit lairs.

## Gaucin

Southwest of Ronda, the A-369 leads to the prettiest of the pueblos, Gaucin. These barren mountainscapes proved ideal hiding places for fugitive Moors during the conquest, and many of the villages here bear the prefix 'Ben' – Benadolid, Benalauria, Benarraba – from the Arabic *ibn* ('son of'). Gaucin is now a sizeable artists' colony, with one excellent hotel, the Casablanca, and an equally excellent restaurant and upmarket country hostel, the stylish La Fructuosa.

## Casares

Below Gaucin, on another peak between the village and the coast, is tiny Casares.

Another classic tangle of whitewashed alleys on a mountain peak, it is notable chiefly as the birthplace of Blas Infante, the founder of the Andalucismo regional autonomy movement in the 1930s.

## Jimena de la Frontera

West beyond Gaucin, before the sierras flatten out towards Gibraltar, is the pleasant hill town of Jimena de la Frontera, with another fortress from the centuries of the Reconquest, two good hotels (El Anon, notably) and a burgeoning international arts festival in August that is fast becoming the envy of the pueblos.

The rooftops of Grazalema, the most dramatic pueblo blanco and wettest town in Spain

# Los Bandoleros (Bandits)

As recently as the 1950s the mountains of the Serrania de Ronda were still known as bandit country, although these bandits were a somewhat different breed from the highwaymen of the 18th and 19th centuries. The treacherous mountain routes between Algeciras and Gibraltar and the cities of Seville, Málaga and Granada had long been favoured by *contrabandistas*, smugglers, bringing illicit supplies ashore and spiriting them through the high mountain passes. The practice continues today, particularly in the use of high-speed boats to bring contraband cigarettes and alcohol, as well as drugs and even people, into Spain. In the 1950s, the bandits shared the mountain paths with fugitive 'Reds', soldiers of the defeated Republican brigades fleeing the vengeance of Franco's henchmen after the Civil War (*see pp100–1*) and eking out an existence at these inhospitable altitudes.

Banditry probably first appeared in Andalucía around the 12th century, where we might date the decisive swing in favour of the Christians during the long centuries of the Reconquest. These first bandits were fugitive Moors fleeing persecution, or at least forced conversion. By the 18th century, with the majority of Moors either assimilated or expelled, the bandits tended to be disenfranchised or disgruntled peasants or disgraced gentry forced to flee into the hills after committing murders or other hanging offences. The Pueblos Blancos were notorious bandit lairs, including Gaucin and, most notorious of all, Olvera, which actually features in a famous saying of the period: 'Kill your man and flee to Olvera.'

Perhaps inevitably, many of these figures acquired a romantic, Robin Hood-like, status, and their system of exacting money from the unwary rich if they ventured unwisely into the

mountains would certainly have struck a welcome chord with the region's poor. One such, José Alloa Tragabuches, was a famous Ronda bullfighter and a pupil of Pedro Romero (see pp78–9). Myths about Tragabuches vary: in one he killed a rival matador and fled justice, while in another he killed an unfaithful wife or girlfriend in a fit of jealous rage and headed for Olvera. Today his handsome cigar-smoking profile adorns the publicity for Ronda's post-modern shrine to new Andalucían cuisine, Tragabuches restaurant (his spirit may yet return to haunt it).

Another bandit, José María Hinojosa Cabacho, nicknamed El Tempranillo, was a media legend in his own time, and was even given to issuing his own press releases, once declaring that while the king might rule Spain, El Tempranillo ruled the sierras. When wealthy northern Europeans began to tour

Andalucía in the 19th century, figures such as El Tempranillo were even contacted by rich tourists willing to pay for the thrill of being 'held up' by a bona fide bandit. And when El Tempranillo married a young woman from (and in) Grazalema, the authorities are said to have turned a blind eye while the nuptials took place.

The romantic form of banditry began to die out in the mid-19th century, due largely to drastic measures taken by the state. However, an ex-urban myth still surfaces from time to time of a former (and, presumably, rather aged) 'Red' found still hiding out in the sierras, and unaware that the Civil War has come to an end.

Facing page: The barren Serrania mountains
Above: Entrance to the Bandit Museum in Ronda

# Walk: Benaoján to Jimera de Libar

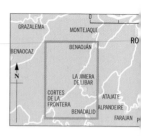

This spectacular walk along the rio Guadiaro valley is one of the most accessible off-road walks in the region, suitable for a morning or shady late afternoon walk, and with transport and refreshment options at either end.
*Allow 2–3 hours.*

*Benaoján is accessible from Ronda by bus, rail or a gentle 6km (3.75 mile) downhill track through farmland. Ideally this should be a morning walk begun from Benaoján, with the added proviso that the route, on rough paths above the riverbed, should not be attempted in inclement weather or by the uncertain solo walker. The perfect itinerary, possible from either starting point, would either end or pause for lunch at Benaoján's El Molino hotel's lovely garden restaurant, under willows by a waterfall feeding the rio Guadiaro.*

The entrance to El Gato cave system just outside Benaoján

## 1 Benaoján Station

The route proper begins at and across the traffic level crossing at the far end of Benaoján station. Signs for the path lead right, off the road and into open countryside.

## 2 Riverside Track

You'll find yourself on a rough but substantial dirt track following the river to your right and with the Ronda–Algeciras railway line elevated above it, also on your right. The path rises and falls from a few feet to a hundred or so feet above the riverbank, with no major diversions and only two minor tributaries to ford by stepping stone or rudimentary wood bridge. *Halfway through the route, just past a ruined farmhouse on the left, you'll be faced by a fork, but in fact both routes continue on to the destination.*

## 3 Cueva de la Pileta

This is an idler's walk, with plenty of spots to stop for a snack or breather, or to take in the fantastic mountain views (including the entrance to the Cueva de la Pileta cave system above the

Benaoján–Jimera road, high above you). These primeval hillsides, awash in cistus and irises in spring, were once home to bandits (*see pp82–3*) and much of the terrain has been undisturbed for millions of years.

### 4 Quercus Restaurant

Nearing Jimera, the path passes a derelict riverside café and then crosses the tracks, to pass behind the Quercus restaurant (also recommended) on the Jimera railway platform.
*Rail connections can be used to return to Benaoján or Ronda for lunch (although currently not onward to Cortes and the Gecko, but it's worth a cab). Train times can change, so consult an up-to-date RENFE timetable.*

*There are also a number of extensions, one a diversion of a matter of minutes, two others long enough to extend this route into a full day ramble, worth considering before you plan your itinerary.*

### 5 Estación Cortes de la Frontera

From Jimera, you can continue on a slightly shorter riverside hike to Estación Cortes de la Frontera and its riverside Hotel El Gecko.
*Allow 2.5 hours extra.*

### 6 El Gato

Just outside Benaoján on the road towards Ronda, accessible across the rail line, is the dramatic El Gato cave system, its entrance open to all (*free*), but its depths the preserve of the experienced cave diver.

### 7 La Venta Vega

Serious *senderistas* (walkers) might also want to consider prefacing the Benaoján–Jimera stretch with the stroll from La Venta Vega restaurant on the Seville road downhill (after the first kilometre) through breathtaking mountain passes and valleys to Benaoján itself.
*Allow 2.5 hours extra.*

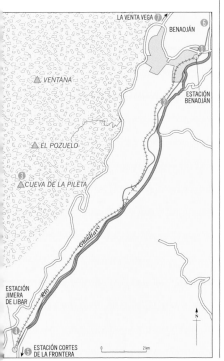

# Parque Natural Sierra de Grazalema

The Parque Natural Sierra de Grazalema is one of the wildest nature reserves in Andalucía, but also one of the most accessible. Its position, equidistant between Atlantic and Mediterranean, has influenced its geology, flora and fauna, and the presence of centres of habitation such as the Pueblos Blancos has brought farmers, hunters and tourists closer than to any other parque natural in Andalucía. This also, in 1984, inspired the declaration of the parque natural, to protect the region from unwanted incursions that might threaten its ecosystem.

The park comprises 52,000 hectares (128,500 acres) stretching between the rios Majaceite, Guadalete and Guadiaro, and the villages of Grazalema itself, Zahara, Villaluenga, Ubrique, Cortes de la Frontera and Ronda. It is one of just 20 such parks in Andalucía, covering a total of 1.4 million hectares (3,460,000 acres), but one of the very few to have imposed visiting restrictions on parts of the reserve.

Visitors will start noticing signs for the park, which straddles both Cádiz and Málaga provinces, as far afield as Ronda, Cortes, Algodonales and El Bosque.

Some of the more spectacular parts of the park are only accessible by vehicle, although the region's public transport, by road or rail, does connect such destinations as Benaoján, Cortes, Ubrique, El Bosque, Algodonales and Grazalema itself. A number of private travel companies in the larger Pueblos Blancos also organise tours and expeditions through the park. The walking and four-wheeler routes between Grazalema and Zahara – especially in the area of the Garganta Verde ('Green Throat') gorge popular with canyoners – are the most heavily policed. These areas are particularly at risk from fire in high season, from disturbance during the breeding season for rare species (when some raptors and snakes may attack anyone or anything approaching their nests) or simply from accidental or careless damage. As well as taking care of rubbish, fires and noise, visitors are asked to remain on marked paths and not disturb anything – rock, plant, tree – they see. Permits are free but limited, and issued by three offices, in El Bosque, Cortes and Grazalema (see opposite).

Local tourism offices and hotels can advise on routes and conditions and what you are likely to see depending on the season.

While rarer inhabitants, such as the golden eagle, are only seen occasionally, it's possible to glimpse kestrels, vultures, owls, otters and other water reptiles, lizards, snakes and, in the highest reaches, even ibex vaulting among the crags. A more modest, if ubiquitous, star of the park's flora and fauna is *abies pinsapo*, the pinsapo pine, found only here in the Serrania de Ronda and in north Africa, as well as a wealth of other pines, rock plants, dwarf orchid, cyclamen and antirrhinum, and the equally ubiquitous holm oak, cistus and broom.

## Information

Two Grazalema-based agencies, Horizon (*Tel: 956 13 23 63*) and Pinzapo (*Tel: 65 13 21 66*) offer various tours and activities inside the park, including accredited guides to the more limited areas.

*Oficina de Información del Parque El Bosque, Avenida de la Diputación. Tel: 956 72 70 29.*

*Información Turística Grazalema, Plaza de España. Tel: 956 13 22 25.*

*Centro de Interpretación de la Naturaleza Cortes, Avenida de la Democracia. Tel: 952 15 43 45.*

The wilder parts of Grazalema's park are tightly controlled by park authorities

# Costa del Sol

Although it has been a synonym for the worst excesses of holiday development for more than a quarter century, it would be snobbish and lazy simply to dismiss the Costa del Sol out of hand. Parts are blighted by unregulated sprawl, but the 21st-century first-time visitor may be surprised at how much of it remains free of the intense high-rise development seen in places such as Benidorm. A new breed of tourist, moneyed and, often as not, headed for the lush green golf courses that dot the 'Costa del Golf', as it is also known, is nurturing a new breed of tourism – one that actually speaks Spanish.

Marbella palms

The Costa del Sol stretches from La Linea de la Concepción, on the border with Gibraltar and today a grim suburb of the Rock, to Málaga and the few small beach resorts to its east.

### Estepona

The first stop of note, this is a fairly low-key resort with a big expatriate community, but still visibly and verbally a working Spanish town. Away from the busy seafront, much of the town centre is pedestrian, with lateral boulevards and cobbled streets that run between two pleasant squares, Plaza las Flores and Plaza Arces. The town has a busy modernist Plaza de Toros, which also hosts occasional concerts given by international artists touring Spain, and below it by the lighthouse a Puerto Deportivo whose bars and clubs are less desperately trendy than those in Puerto Banús. It has an interesting Sunday market (as does nearby Manilva) with

crafts and the odd stall offering fake Rolexes. Casares and the nearer Pueblos Blancos (*see pp80–1*) are a short drive or bus ride north.

### San Pedro de Alcantara

Landlocked a kilometre away from its beach en route to Marbella, this is actually a pleasant little Spanish town, with pedestrian streets and the handsome Plaza de la Iglesia where townsfolk promenade. It is also the main shopping centre for the booming *urbanizaciones*, gated housing developments, nearby, with multilingual bookshops and newsstands, restaurants and stores. San Pedro is also the main turn-off for Ronda and Seville (buses can get very busy, even full, in high season).

Marbella and Puerto Banús are covered in the pages which follow, as is the city of Málaga, but there are still a couple of interesting stops on the costa.

Fuengirola is, unfortunately, not one of them, although it is a stopping-off point for the pretty interior town of Mijas and, for non-drivers, the terminus station for Málaga's half-hourly coastal train service (with a stop at the airport).

### Torremolinos

Torremolinos is currently living down a reputation as a beer and beach resort, and the authorities are following Marbella's model in town gentrification, with replanted squares and pedestrian areas. It remains a big nightlife resort,

however, and after Sitges is probably the biggest gay resort in Spain, with its own Gay Pride celebrations each June and numerous friendly gay and drag bars on calle de Nogueras.

### Benalmadena

Many of Torremolinos's quieter tourist attractions, such as Sea Life and the Tivoli *parque tematico* (theme park), are in this satellite town, which has a cable-car system up into the hills overlooking the town. The pueblo proper of Benalmadena, a few kilometres inland, is surprisingly unspoilt.

Marbella's paseo maritimo, a favourite stroll for townsfolk and visitors alike

# Marbella and Puerto Banús

Marbella is the most fascinating of Andalucía's Mediterranean cities, although not always for the right reasons. It became a magnet for the jet set in the late 1950s and early 1960s, and with the advent of mass market travel established itself as perhaps the most high-class resort on Spain's Mediterranean littoral. The intervening decades have been something of a rollercoaster ride for the resort and its smaller sibling, the marina playground of Puerto Banús 4km to the west.

Marbella's medieval fortifications

Spain's laid-back attitude to international extradition treaties at this time also made it a haven for north European criminals and their booty – as well, alas, as their murderous feuds. Marbella's reputation nosedived after a series of particularly gruesome murders, and only in recent decades has it begun to claw back some of its earlier glamour. It is a place where you can buy Fabergé eggs and Ferregamo ballgowns, but also where bodies can turn up in the most unexpected places. At times it resembles Beverly Hills, but at others, Al Capone's New York.

Two men made modern-day Marbella: Prince Alfonso von Hohenlohe, an Austrian aristocrat with Mexican connections who built the Marbella Club Hotel in the 1950s, and the former mayor, controversial right-wing business tycoon and boss of Atletico Madrid football club Jesus Gil y Gil, who came to power in 1991. One of Gil's more notorious claims is that Spain was 'better off under Franco', which might give a measure of his political philosophy.

Hohenlohe, whose name now graces an excellent red wine, Principe Alfonso, produced at his Las Monjas vineyards outside Ronda (you can visit – there's even a restaurant), was the man who brought the jet set to Marbella. His Marbella Club Hotel still stands on the beach of its 'Golden Mile', the million-euro-plus villa zone, where more discreet money tends to stay away from the flashbulbs that illuminate its garish neighbour, Puerto Banús. The jet set long ago moved on. Marbella's newer money prefers to stay behind the tall walls of its security-guarded villas, where it can read its imported Russian newspapers in peace.

Gil, for his part, oversaw a drastic refit for the ailing resort, often at the cost of finer sensibilities such as planning committees, and has enthusiastically pursued his own business interests inside and outside the city. (His modest *pied-à-terre* is at the far end of Marbella's main drag, Avenida Ricardo Soriano, handy for the drive-in Burger King.) Gil also introduced zero-tolerance policies to rid the city of many of its shadier figures, but also the simply destitute. It is this extreme contrast between wealth and poverty that gives Marbella its air of decadence.

Despite this, or perhaps thanks to it, Marbella remains an immensely attractive place to visit. Gil's plans gave Marbella a particularly handsome seafront promenade, now lined with restaurants, and its lovely old Alameda, shaded by aged palms, now gives on to a hi-tech *rambla* decorated with Salvador Dali bronzes.

### Where to Stay

Curiously for such a smart resort, Marbella has few good hotels in its centre. The emetic pink Fuerte, overlooking the beach at the east end of

Soriano, is a pleasant but pricey five-star with all amenities, but most mid-range hotels are indifferent and plagued by traffic noise. An exception is the stylish La Morada Mas Hermosa in the *casco antiguo* (*see p178 for Marbella hotels*).

### Casco Antiguo (Old Town)

The *casco antiguo* (old town) has been exquisitely refurbished, nowhere more so than in Plaza de los Naranjos (square of the orange trees), where the 17th-century *ayuntamiento* building overlooks some of the priciest bars in town. In fact, the whitewashed alleys and squares of the *casco* would give any of the Pueblos Blancos a run for their money, as would some of its restaurants, such as the international La Comedia.

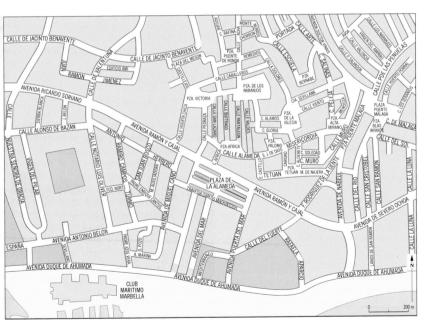

The leafy Alameda in Marbella's heart

### Disco 2000

The southern tip of the *casco* conceals a rather less obvious cultural monument, possibly the hippest record store in Andalucía. While small, it has a range extending beyond international, folk, flamenco and dance to encompass contemporary jazz and the avant-garde, and is certainly the only place in Andalucía to find John Cage or Philip Glass. *Avenida Ricardo Soriano.*

### Iglesia de la Encarnación

Some of Marbella's cultural icons are concealed in the *casco*, not least the impressive 16th-century Iglesia de la Encarnación, in its own plaza a few blocks east of Plaza de los Naranjos. *Plaza de la Iglesia. Open: 8am–2pm & 5–8pm. Free.*

### Museo Bonsai

Marbella has what is thought to be Spain's only bonsai museum, with over 150 small but perfectly formed species on display.

*Arroyo de la Represa. Open: daily 10am–1.30pm & 4–8pm. Admission charge.*

### Museo del Grabado Contemporáneo

Hidden in an alleyway behind the Iglesia de la Encarnación is the small but impressive Museum of Contemporary Prints, housed in a Renaissance mansion originally built as a hospital. It has a sizeable collection of Mirós, some smaller works by Picasso, and a feisty policy of showcasing contemporary art. The building itself, on four floors, is worth the entry alone and is being expanded. The museum is close by the remnants of the Moorish ramparts to the city.

*Calle Hospital Bazán. Open: Mon–Fri 10am–2pm & 6–9pm. Admission charge.*

### Puerto Banús

When Marbella wants to party, or shop, it heads west for Puerto Banús, although for some this may still beg the question: why? For years its windswept, empty shopping malls and equally deserted

The Plaza de los Naranjos, the prettiest square in the beautiful casco antiguo

luxury apartment blocks looked as though they had been visited by a science-fiction disaster, although now mall staples such as Body Shop are setting up their stalls here.

The **marina** itself has long been a tourist attraction, although mainly for gawpers naively expecting a glimpse of Bruce Willis or Rod Stewart, as the signed celebrity photos in the bars seem to promise. The boats are fun to look at (at any time, there must be half a billion euros moored in Puerto Banús), as are their owners, and there are numerous good if expensive seafood, American and even an Indian restaurant on the quay. But Puerto Banús still has the slightly dislocated air of something that has just landed here from outer space.

Most visitors will be laden with evidence of the main reason to visit: bags from the vast **El Corte Inglés** department store that looms over the rear of the marina. Possibly the biggest Corte Inglés ('English cut', a tailoring term) store outside Madrid and Barcelona, this boasts a small children's funfair and its own bus station.

An alternative form of transport to Marbella in season is the regular sea bus leaving from the marina.

Puerto Banús, playground to the rich, and its marina

# Málaga

Andalucía's second largest city after Seville, with a population of over half a million, Málaga is the least developed for tourism of all Andalucía's cities. Yet it is the main (air)port of entry for visitors, the administrative centre for most government agencies, and the place where you will find overseas consulates or their representatives. Sometimes it can seem that if anything – a computer, car part or machine – goes wrong in southern Andalucía, it has to be sent to Málaga.

Málaga's one-armed lady

Like virtually every hub airport in the Mediterranean basin, Málaga is a place where visitors land and find themselves immediately bussed elsewhere. Few bother to visit except when passing by again en route home, but this sometimes daunting industrial metropolis has a rich and vibrant culture and history.

Málaga's history stretches back to the Phoenicians, who established it as a key Mediterranean port, a role it has kept through Moorish and Christian rule until the present day. The Phoenicians also introduced viniculture, which blossomed with the city's sweet and fortified wines, but the industry was devastated by the 19th-century phylloxera epidemic. (The Larios family did better with their Málaga-distilled gin, which still beats famous British brands in blindfold tests.)

The city gave Spain and indeed the 20th century its most famous painter, Picasso, and it was the second most fought-over Republican bulwark after Barcelona during the Civil War. It is also the most unapologetically Spanish of Andalucía's cities, with a lively university and gay community, and a major August feria that requires reserves of stamina if it is to be survived.

The cathedral and the student cafés around the Casa Natal de Picasso are good places to find outdoor bars and restaurants. Try also the nearby Malagueta beachfront for bars and fish restaurants.

### Alcazaba

As befits a city of Málaga's status, it has some impressive archaeological sites. The Alcazaba starts at the site of a recently discovered Roman theatre and climbs through Moorish and later stages to the Gibralfaro castle at the top of its hill. Bafflingly, the *parador* in its grounds resembles a low-rise motel with service to match and should be avoided. *Open: Wed–Mon 9.30am–6.30pm. Closed: Tue. Free.*

The Alcazaba seen from the Alameda

### Casa Natal de Picasso and Museo Picasso

Picasso may have pointedly stayed away from Franco's Spain, and refused to allow the iconic *Guernica* to be displayed here in his lifetime, but the city has been gradually coaxing his memory back home. The Casa Natal de Picasso has been open as a museum and archive for some time, and although its Picassos are few, and minor, it is also used as a showcase for contemporary Málagueñan and Spanish art. More recently, the Museo Picasso opened a few blocks south to do justice to his work with a rotating collection of his pieces.
*Casa Natal de Picasso, Plaza de la Merced. Open: Mon–Sat 10am–2pm & 6–8pm, Sun 10am–2pm. Free.*
*Museo Picasso, calle San Agustin. Open: Mon–Sat 10am–2pm & 6–8pm, Sun 10am–2pm. Free.*

### Catedral

Málaga's cathedral is low on architectural detail but big on imposing presence: it's the size of a small mountain. A hotchpotch of Gothic, Renaissance and Baroque, it is made odder by the absence of one of its towers (funds were diverted to Spain's war chest), which earned it the nickname La Manquita, the One-Armed Lady.
*Calle Molina Lario. Open: Mon–Sat 10am–6.45pm. Admission charge.*

# Picasso

Few artists can hope to generate controversies extending over two centuries, but more than 125 years after his birth Pablo Ruiz Picasso still manages to upset people's notions of what constitutes art.

Picasso was born in Málaga's Plaza de la Merced in 1881 to artistic parents – his father was a teacher, and it was under his influence that Picasso began painting in his early teens. As even his mid-teen self-portraits and other exercises – most of them conventional representational works – showed, he had a precocious skill and eye for the different.

His father was appointed to Barcelona's La Lonja art school in 1895, and Picasso was accepted as an exceptional student the following year. Within a matter of years he had been adopted as the mascot of Barcelona's *modernista* avant-garde that met at the Els Quatre Gats (Four Cats) bar. By 1897, he was studying at the Royal Academy in Madrid and already attracting critical attention. Toulouse-Lautrec and Cézanne were influences on his work, and the latter would continue to influence him along with Gauguin and other fauvists (primitives).

Picasso began his first distinctive work, what was later called his 'blue period', in 1901, when he was barely 20, a period typified by works such as *The Old Guitarist* (1903). Like the subsequent 'rose period', while accurate in terms of material and chronologically verifiable, this was not part of a traditional career trajectory, of an artist experimenting or developing. Picasso already knew what he wanted to do, and how he wanted to portray things. Like his next, almost literally shattering, change of

technique, these were simply methods for realising what he saw.

The drastic departure from tradition, one that still startles art historians, came in 1907 with *Les Demoiselles d'Avignon*, depicting a group of semi-naked bathers composed as in classical portraiture. These figures, however, took their form from pre-Christian Iberian statuary, African sculpture and the influences of Cézanne and Gauguin, and fused them in a shocking new way that prefigured cubism, vorticism and many other 20th-century schools of art.

With Georges Braque and fellow countryman Juan Gris, Picasso expanded this fractured look at representation by introducing found objects – newspaper, string, and other workaday materials – into a collage that would blossom into full-blown sculpture.

During the 1920s, now based in Paris, Picasso produced some of his most famous cubist pieces, such as *Three Musicians* (1921), while also working on studies of monumental, primitive figures, notably the *Deux Femmes Courant sur la Plage* (1922). He also began to introduce mythical icons – minotaurs, bulls, horses – into his work. These themes would come to the fore in his paintings and etchings from the 1930s, most famously in 1936 in *Guernica*, his response to the German bombing of the Basque town of Gernika, a Republican stronghold, at the behest of Franco's Falangists.

Picasso moved to Antibes in the south of France following the Second World War, where he continued to produce paintings, line drawings, ceramics and sculptures until his death in 1973.

Facing page: Picasso's birthplace in Plaza de la Merced
Left: Pablo Ruiz Picasso

# Walk: El Chorro

This short but dramatic walk is only 30 minutes by car or train from Málaga and easily accessible from Ronda, Antequera or Ardales. It takes in one of the most striking sights in Andalucía, the Camino del Rey – a suspended walkway clinging to the sheer cliffs one hundred feet or so above the rio Guadalhorce. This is in fact a man-made channel, built through the El Chorro gorge in the 1920s as part of the rio Guadalhorce hydroelectric system, inaugurated in 1921 by King Alfonso XIII, who walked the length of the walkway and gave it its nickname.

This can be an extremely dangerous adventure. The suspended walkway has been falling apart for decades, and is officially off-limits to the public. As well as following guide instructions, it is advisable to take local advice, and even to contact local travel companies about guided tours around the safer parts of the Camino and El Chorro.
*This simpler and safer walk begins at El Chorro railway station on the Bobadilla–*

*The Camino del Rey walkway*

*Málaga line. Not all trains stop here, but in summer El Chorro's campsites and guest houses are busy enough to ensure that most do, and off-season a* parada solicitada *(request stop) system operates. The walk is 10km (6.2 miles) so allow 3 hours.*

## 1 El Chorro station
Leaving the station, follow the signposted road to Pantano (reservoir) de Guadalhorce, roughly 8km (5 miles) west of the station and hydroelectric system. *When the road hits a T-junction turn right, following the sign for the Mirador restaurant, 2km (1.2 miles) on.*

## 2 Mirador restaurant
The aptly named Mirador (viewpoint) overlooks the several lakes and *embalses* (reservoirs) formed by the Guadalhorce, Guadalteba and other rivers in this mountainous area.
*A well-used dirt path from the restaurant leads a further 2km (1.2 miles) downhill to an abandoned hydroelectric plant.*

### 3  Gorge entrance

This plant, part of the Guadalhorce system, lies at the entrance to the gorge and the Camino. The route onwards is marked 'No Entry', although you may encounter others exploring the entrance to the walkway.

*Even with expert mountaineering guidance, this is only for those with climbing skills and a steely head for heights. It is far safer simply to enjoy the views, head back or consider a couple of alternative routes.*

### 4  Riverside path

A far safer option, given good weather, is to return to El Chorro railway station and take the riverside pathway leading off from there. *2km (1.2 miles).*

### 5  Ruinas de Bobastro

A more strenuous alternative is to take the left turning, halfway to the Mirador junction from the station, signposted for the Ruinas de Bobastro 4km (2.48 miles) away, where the remains of the 9th-century fort built by bandit Ibn Hafsun can be seen. Like most of the El Chorro routes, this is a one-way, dead-end route.

*Several maps cover El Chorro and environs, to varying degree and availability. The Michelin Andalucía 446 is widely available, but has little detail of the gorge itself. Spain's Instituto Geografico Nacional issues a range of maps up to 1:50,000 and beyond. The LTC map store (Avenida Menéndez Pelayo 42–44 Seville; tel: 954 42 59 64; email: ltc-mapas@sp-editores.es) can help with requirements.*

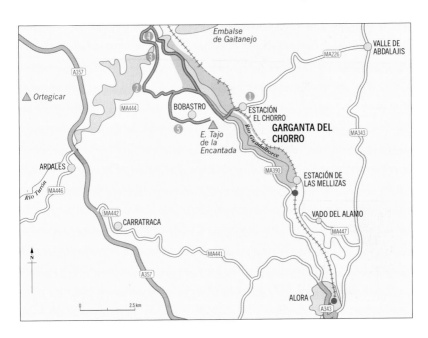

The causes of the Civil War that killed nearly half a million people in Spain during 1936–9 can be traced back to the successive Carlist Wars of the 18th century or the failed attempts to introduce a democratic republic in to this notoriously plutocratic society.

The loss of Spain's colonies in the 19th century undermined the economy, as did the phylloxera epidemic of the 1870s, which destroyed vineyards across Europe. Anarchists and others had been fomenting dissent throughout the second half of the 19th century, sparking strikes and occupations, usually put down brutally by the armed forces. By the start of the 20th century, Spain was already on the boil.

Spain's workers took to the nascent trades union movement at the turn of that century with a gusto unseen elsewhere in Europe. They formed rival political unions with vast memberships, some of which, such as the anarchist CNT, exist (in altered form) today. The first taste of what was to come broke out in Barcelona in 1909, during the *Setmana Tragica* (tragic week), when a general strike turned into an uprising against the state and the church, which the rioters saw as culpable in maintaining their misery.

Spain remained neutral during the First World War, but with an economy spiralling into recession. Following what seems to have been a fairly common rule of 'When in doubt, stage a military coup', the powers that be appointed General Primo de Rivera, from Jerez, as head of its latest dictatorship. Rivera survived until 1930 and the great Ibero-American Exhibition in Seville, which coincided with the Wall Street Crash and worldwide recession.

Spain finally got a working republic in 1931, a coalition of anarchists, communists, socialists and liberals. This fractured alliance would be their undoing, not least when the right-wing Falangists, formed in 1926 and with Francisco Franco y Bahamonde as nominal head, decided to take things into their hands. On 17 July 1936 General Franco led his garrison in Morocco in an open rebellion, airlifted his men to Seville, took the city and declared himself El Caudillo (the leader). The Republicans, disorganised and riven by factional in-fighting, were no match for the 'Nationalists' and their allies in the Italian and German fascist movements, who aided El Caudillo with, for example, the blanket bombing of Gernika (Guernica).

Despite the superior firepower of the Nationalists, the Republicans fought on, most notably in Madrid, Barcelona and Málaga, for three years. The Republican struggle attracted support from overseas in the form of the International Brigades, who arrived in their hundreds from Britain, the USA and elsewhere. Madrid was the last city to fall, in March 1939, and Franco declared a Nationalist victory in April.

Both sides committed terrible atrocities during the Civil War – Barcelona was the site of horrendous anti-clerical riots – and evidence of these, in particular mass revenge killings by Nationalists, is still being unearthed in the 21st century. Yet, however one regards it, the Civil War was and remains a simple struggle between democracy and tyranny. Unfortunately for two generations of Spanish people, tyranny won.

Facing page: Málaga's Port Authority building was a key bomb target for fascist planes
Left: Ronda's Puente Nuevo was used as a prison during the Civil War

# Las Alpujarras

These tall and steep mountain valleys south of Granada comprise one of the most geographically and culturally distinct regions of Andalucía. Their remote villages became natural refuges for Moors fleeing the forces of the Reconquest, and their resistance to progress made them a natural destination for 19th-century Romantic visitors, most famously the English travel writer Richard Ford.

Orgiva church

Today they offer a natural refuge for a different kind of fugitive, and a different kind of romantic. For the past three or so decades, the Alpujarras have been home to north European dropouts, who live in communal farms and tepee communities off the beaten track, and whose presence has probably helped sustain mountain villages which might have otherwise been abandoned, as has happened elsewhere in Andalucía. For somewhat longer, they have also attracted romantics in the footsteps of Ford: most notably, the writer Gerald Brenan, and most recently Chris Stewart, whose books *Driving Over Lemons* and *A Parrot in the Pepper Tree* have made the town of Órgiva and its environs world famous.

When Brenan arrived, the busy market town of Órgiva was still a gathering of tiny hamlets connected, if at all, by mountain tracks. The villages have changed drastically since Brenan complained in *South from Granada* of the surly welcome and populous bedbugs he encountered, travelling after the First World War, in the 'airless and shut-in' Alpujarran villages. Yet geography and communications have conspired to keep the Alpujarras nearer to the beginning of the 20th century than the 21st.

Few roads, and still fewer public transport routes, penetrate the mountains, which are divided into the 'High' and 'Low' Alpujarras, above and below the core towns of Lanjarón and Órgiva. They are also divided east–west, across the valleys that take the rios Lanjarón and Ugíjar to the sea.

The remoteness that attracted Moorish refugees inspired the distinctive Berber architecture of the villages, with their flat, often stone, roofs, and stone and clay walls (only recently painted white over the traditional brown). It also informed the types of trade that flourished in the mountains: apart from agriculture and services, most businesses have been generated in the eccentric forms of tourism, including a Tibetan Buddhist temple and a mountain-spring spa, that have developed here.

Most notably, however, the Alpujarras' proximity to the great Moorish culture of Granada and, to a lesser extent, the Caliphate of Córdoba, puts them in the

The spa town of Lanjarón, source of Spain's most popular bottled water

foothills of Granada's Moorish history. After Granada fell to the Christians in 1492 (the same year Colón sailed), the last Moorish king, Boabdil, was 'given' the Alpujarras as his personal fiefdom. The pass south of Granada where he is said to have paused for a last glimpse of his fallen kingdom is known as Puerto del Suspiro del Moro (the Moor's Last Sigh). Boabdil is believed to have died around 1538, his miniature Moorish kingdom lasting barely 30 years longer. Following a doomed uprising in the Alpujarras, the final Mudéjars, those 'allowed to stay', were either expelled or forcibly converted. Two Moorish households were kept in each village to help maintain the agricultural marvel that the Moors wrought in the Alpujarra valleys, but the system soon slipped into a decline that has only begun to be reversed in recent decades.

# Lanjarón, Órgiva and Beyond

Some seventy pueblos, most of them hamlets, make up the Alpujarras, most famously the spa town of Lanjarón and the agricultural centre of Órgiva. These constitute the Lower Alpujarras, while above them Bubión and Capileira are the centres of habitation of the High Alpujarras. A scant bus service (one bus daily from Granada, three between the pueblos) follows the one highway connecting the Alpujarras as far as Ugíjar.

*For the bus service tel: 958 18 50 10.*

*Espantabrujas, 'witch-scarers', are common in mountain villages*

### Lanjarón

Famed throughout Spain as the source of the bottled spring water sold in every Spanish supermarket, Lanjarón has been a centre of population and a renowned spa since Roman times. The *balneario*, or spa, is on its one main street, Avenida Andalucía, and in summer months throngs with people (often sent by the Spanish health system) taking its treatments. The presence of the spa has ensured that plenty of accommodation is available, most of it on Avenida Andalucía. While the mountain setting is pleasant, there is little else to Lanjarón, apart from some good walks into the hills. The fact that its sole highway is also the A-348 connecting the Low Alpujarras villages gives it the air of a one-strip town.

### Órgiva

Also known as Órjiva, this bustling town is the commercial centre of the Alpujarras, scene of a busy Thursday market that attracts farmers and hippies alike from surrounding villages. (There's also a lively daily covered market.) Órgiva still boasts the vestigial remnants of a Moorish palace, but its main attraction is the Baroque **Iglesia de Nuestra Señora de la Expectación**. Drivers should note that Órgiva's petrol station is the last until Cadiar or Ugíjar.
*Iglesia de Nuestra Señora de la Expectación, Plaza Mayor. Open: daily 9am–2pm. Free.*

### High Alpujarras

As this would suggest, Órgiva in particular is an excellent base for exploring further into the Alpujarras. Northeast of Órgiva lie **Bubión** and **Capileira**, among the highest of the High Alpujarras, small villages clinging to mountainsides accessible only by path. Bubión is also a good base for horse trekking into the mountains with agencies such as Dallas Ranch (*tel: 958 76 30 39*). **Pampaneira**, the first village on the route up to Capileira, is also home to the aforementioned Tibetan

Buddhist monastery of **Osel Ling**. The monastery (*open: daily 3–6pm*) has a spectacular setting on a track above the village, and can even offer simple accommodation for visitors and those attending courses and lectures there. *Enquiries: tel: 958 34 31 34.*

## Eastern Low Alpujarras

The A-348 east continues on to the central towns of the eastern Low Alpujarras, Cadiar, Valor and Ugíjar. **Cadiar** is the market centre of this region of the Alpujarras, with a twice monthly market in its tiny town square. The Cadiar–Valor road passes the still tiny hamlet of **Yegen**, where Gerald Brenan set up home in the 1920s, and where a small plaque identifies his house near the fountain at the centre of the village. The even smaller hamlet of **Valor** was the scene of some of the fiercest Moorish uprisings against the Christians, an event marked every September when townsfolk stage a rematch during their feria (dates vary). **Ugíjar**, teetering at the border of Granada's Alpujarras and those in the arid region of Almería, is another market town and a centre for good hill walking.

These mountain villages are recommended to walkers with or without their own transport, suitably armed with maps and an up-to-date bus timetable.

Órgiva's town centre gears up for market day

# Walk: Capileira and the High Alpujarras

This is one of the easier walks in the High Alpujarras, with various options for detours off the main route. It starts at the centre of the pretty mountain village of Capileira – within easy striking distance of Órgiva and a possible base itself – and can be pursued as far as mood, stamina or weather dictate. It also begins at above 1,400m (4,593ft) above sea level, with only a minimal climb up the Poqueira Gorge to the power station above it.

*Allow half a day or less.*

### 1 Capileira

The walk begins in the village centre, heading downhill towards the river. The lowest bridge crosses the river outside the village and is named on some maps Puente Chiscar. This will lead you up through the steep cultivated hillsides above Capileira.

### 2 Poqueira Gorge

The path continues for 4km (2.5 miles) or so (*on this terrain, estimate a walking duration of 1.5 hours for this*), before you meet the path leading up the Poqueira Gorge to the hydroelectric power station installed many years ago on the rio Poqueira.

### 3 Return to Capileira

From here you have a variety of options. Crossing over the river you'll encounter a dirt path that will lead you back down to Capileira. Continue up to the hydroelectric plant and a path at a fork below it will also lead you back down to Capileira.

### Other Walks from Capileira

Alternatively, there are signposted walks from the Capileira bridges to the tiny neighbouring hamlet of **Carataunas** (*1 hour*), or the larger neighbour **Pampaneira** (*3 hours*), with its option of visiting the **Osel Ling** Tibetan Buddhist monastery (*see p105*). A simple stroll will also take you down into **Órgiva** (*45 mins*), with the option of walking back or taking one of the intra-village buses.

More strenuous hikes to remoter destinations such as **Trevelez** (*5 hours*) are also possible from Capileira. With expert guidance and equipment, Capileira can also be used as a base for an attempt on **Mulhacén**, the highest 3,480m (11,417ft) peak in the entire Iberian peninsula. This is best done over a period of days, with local accommodation arranged from Capileira or Órgiva. Every year on 5 August the sturdier villagers embark on their annual Romeria, or religious procession, to the hermitage of La Virgen de las Nieves (the Virgin of the Snows),

Capileira and the snows of the Sierra Nevada in the distance

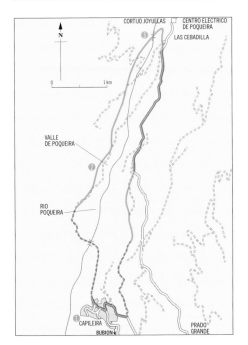

near the summit of Mulhacén. However, this should not be attempted by anyone uncertain about either their ability to climb the largest mountain in Spain or their head for heights.

# Almería Province

It is sobering to consider that, without the arrival of Tariq ibn Zayid and his Berber army in the 8th century, much of Andalucía today would resemble the seared and rocky landscape of its most easterly region.

Almería's dusty interior

Even the water technologies that transformed parts of the southwest into arable oases couldn't change this near-desert. Paradoxically, however, intensive farming under plastic has made Almería the fruit and vegetable basket of Andalucía: so much so that its tourism authorities promote it as *El mar del plastico* (the sea of plastic), which spreads from the coast to the foothills of the Sierra de Gádor. There has been equally intensive tourism development on its coast, at Mojácar and west of the city of Almería itself, while the Parque Natural de Cabo de Gata is one of the most beautiful parks on the Andalucían littoral. The city of Almería itself, although usually low down most visitors' must-see lists, is a little-known treasure, with a *rambla* to rival Barcelona's, a splendid hilltop *alcazaba* (fort), a wealth of extremely handsome architecture and a lively nightlife.

## The Coast

The narrow belt of plain between sea and mountains may be scruffy and often plasticated, but the beaches below it are among the best on the Costa del Sol (here subdivided as the Costa Tropical). To the east, **Mojácar** is a busy resort with a *parador* on its beach (*tel: 951 47 82 50*). The original town, Mojácar

Pueblo, a few kilometres inland, retains much of its charm: this too was inhabited in prehistoric times, and was a major Roman base (now lost). It's also the likely source of the prehistoric Indalo talisman, a stick figure holding a raised archer's bow, originally intended to ward off evil and now replicated on untold tourist souvenirs and logos.

West of the city, **Aguadulce** ('Sweet water') is a thriving marina resort with a small beach. The key resort here is **Roquetas del Mar**, a low-level development that sprawls for kilometres along a wide sandy beach and is best negotiated by the four-person bikes available at points along the beach. Much of Roquetas is signed in numerous northern European languages, and it is an ideal family spot.

## Interior

Accessible by car, bus or train from Almería's smart new Estacion Intermodal, the interior is a different world altogether. The most obvious port of call is **Tabernas** and the Mini Hollywood park where a variety of attractions – Wild West shoot-out and hanging, a bank robbery, and a can-can show – are staged two or three times a day depending on season. There are also restaurants, bars, and a small zoo. There

Water and nautical sculpture where Almería's elegant rambla reaches the sea front

are now three distinct western-themed sites here, with the same opening times. *Mini-Hollywood, A-370 Rioja 10km (6.2 miles). Open: daily, July–Sept 10am–9pm, Oct–June 10am–7pm. Admission charge.*

The more adventurous should head for the beautiful interior town of **Nijar**, with its Mudéjar architecture. The ceramics *talares* (studios) of its Barrio de Atalaya are famed throughout the region. With a car, you can also press on north to pretty mountain towns such as **Bacares** and **Seron**, where it has been known to snow in the winter.

# Almería: the City

The least visited of Andalucía's regional capitals, this thriving port has much to recommend it to the adventurous visitor. It may lack the grand monuments of Seville and Granada, but there's plenty to explore, culture old and new, few of the crowds and hassles of the big cities, and a lively nightlife around its hub, Puerta (gate) de Purchena, with its bars, restaurants and hotels.

City and old town from the sea

Almería, from the Arabic *al-mariya* ('mirror of the sea'), was a major port from the earliest days of the Moorish presence in Andalucía until their expulsion. City and region were severely damaged by an earthquake in 1522 and languished in poverty until the mid-20th century, when efforts began to revive agriculture and develop tourism. Despite the quake, some impressive sights remain, as do handsome examples of later architecture.

## Alcazaba

The Alcazaba fort towers over the old town, but should not be confused with its neighbouring Mirador de San Cristóbal, whose monumental statue can only be visited by an entirely separate route from the city centre. The Alcazaba is on three levels, with ongoing excavations, gardens and water courses and spectacular views from the top, where the circular Torre de la Pólvora (Gunpowder Tower) produces a startling echo wherever you step.

*Calle Almanzor. Open: daily, June–Sept 9am–8.30pm, Oct–May 9am–6.30pm. Admission charge (EU citizens free).*

## Old Town

The old town between the Alcazaba and the port boasts some very fine local architecture with a wealth of eccentric detail. Particularly recommended is **La Plaza Vieja**, also known as Plaza de la Constitución. This beautiful square, like a miniature version of Madrid's Plaza Mayor, has a town hall clock whose chimes echo through the old town (get there for six).

North of the Puerto de Purchena, near the classic Plaza de Toros (bullring), the bizarre modernist **Rambla de Belen** begins to curve down to the seafront and the **Cable Inglés**, an elevated rail head built by the British in the 19th century for the (now defunct) tin industry. Nearby, an enigmatic set of pillars forms a monument to those Almerians who died at the Matthausen concentration camp in the Second World War. (*The Cable will also lead you to the Estación Intermodal bus/rail terminus.*)

## Catedral

Almería's cathedral sits in a stately square and shares its Gothic architecture, and architect Diego de Sileó, with the cathedral at Granada. The Neo-primitive sun icon on its east (dawn-facing) wall has been read as evidence of freemasonry among 16th-century clergy, and is now Almería's official logo.

*Plaza de la Catedral. Open: Mon–Fri 10am–5pm, Sat 10am–1pm. Admission charge.*

### Centro de Arte & Centro Andaluz de la Fotografía

As the Rambla and Matthausen monument attest, Almería also has a taste for modern art. Opposite the Intermodal, the small but impressive new Centro de Arte has frequent exhibits of cutting-edge Spanish art. Housed in a more sedate 18th-century building, the Centro Andaluz de la Fotografía has a similar reputation for contemporary and journalistic photography.

*Centro de Arte, Plaza Barcelona. Open: Mon–Fri 11am–2pm & 6–8pm, Sat 6–8pm, Sun 11am–2pm. Free. Centro Andaluz de la Fotografía, calle Conde Ofalía. Open: Mon–Fri 9am–2pm & 4–9pm. Free.*

(Almería's archaeological museum is currently homeless, but a small display of its treasures is on view at the *Biblioteca Pública, calle Hermanos Machados. Open: Tue–Sat 9am–2pm. Free.*)

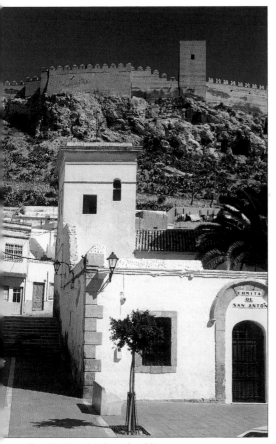

Almería's Alcazaba above the old town

# Walk: Cabo de Gata

Just over half an hour's drive (or regular bus) east from the centre of Almería, Cabo de Gata (Cape of the Cat) – a small resort, geographical promontory, wilderness beach and also a nature reserve – offers various excellent diversions right on the edge of the city. This walk begins at the small, low-rise resort of El Cabo de Gata itself, above the Playa de San Miguel beach, where buses from Almería stop in the ramshackle car park by the Torre de San Miguel martello tower.

The walk circles the Cape of the Cat itself and can either be taken in circular fashion, heading back inland from the Playa de la Fabriquilla, or one way, hopping on one of the regular buses that pass the Cape from the further resort of San José. San José itself, and the picturesque bus ride there, are also worth a detour.

*Allow 6 hours for the circular walk (20km/12.45 miles) and 3 hours for one way only (10km/6.2 miles).*

The Cabo de Gata lighthouse

## 1 Torre de San Miguel
From the martello tower in Cabo de Gata head southeast (left facing the sea) towards the Salinas del Cabo de Gata.

## 2 Salinas del Cabo de Gata
These working salt pans, stretching between the town and Playa de la Fabriquilla, are a haven for indigenous and migratory birds, including, in late August, flocks of flamingoes. The salt pans are home to many other birds, including the avocet and stork, except in winter, when the pans are drained and harvested. Much of the salt industry is based at Las Salinas and La Almadraba de Monteleva, 6km (3.7 miles) from the El Cabo resort.

## 3 Playa de la Fabriquilla
At Playa de la Fabriquilla, the flat plains give way to the Sierra del Cabo hills, few of them above 400m (1,312ft) but dramatic in this setting.

## 4 Faro de Cabo de Gata

The path (bike as well as foot) here joins the coast road and begins to rise up towards the cape itself, with its Faro (lighthouse) de Cabo de Gata perched on 200m-high (656ft) cliffs. There is a visitor information centre here and other facilities, including at least six magnificent *miradors* (viewing platforms), with varied views, a short stroll from the car park. There are two excellent beaches below and beyond the lighthouse. At roughly 12km (7.5 miles) from El Cabo de Gata resort, this is probably the spot for a break and to consider the options.

For those who take their walking seriously, the road back down from the Faro to the Playa de la Fabriquilla heads inland here, and takes a flat detour around the landward side of the salinas.

A lazier option would be to check in El Cabo for times of buses from San José and catch one as it swings through.

## 5 San José

Further along a good but winding clifftop path from the Faro, the resort of San José is a serious day-long hike from El Cabo, although the views are stupendous.

There are numerous other routes inland and west of El Cabo. The best map of the area is produced by Editorial Alpina (Group J126), available in bookshops in El Cabo and Almería. There are also possibilities for sailing, diving and boat excursions from El Cabo: details from the Oficina de Información, Avenida Miramar (*tel: 950 38 02 99*).

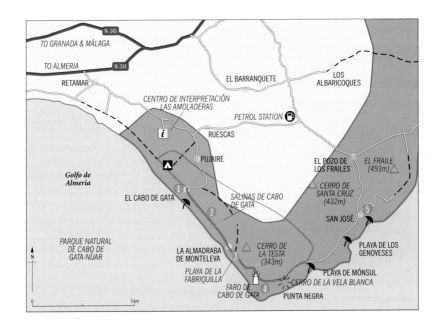

# Granada City and Region

Both the city and region of Granada are set aside from the rest of Andalucía by history, geography and culture. Where Seville is the product of the Reconquest and the Golden Age, Granada is indelibly marked by its Moorish past.

Granada Catedral

The capital, on its arable plain below the Sierra Nevada mountains (home to the only ski resort in Andalucía), is dominated by Spain's most famous Moorish monument, the Alhambra, as well as the neighbouring Albaicín district, which is actually seeing a renaissance in Islamic culture. The defeat of Boabdil in 1492 and the dispersal of the Mudéjars also marked the mountainous regions of the Alpujarras (*see pp102–5*), as well as outlying areas such as the rio Genil valley towards Seville and the cave towns of Guadix and Purullena (*see pp124–5*).

Plaza Nueva at the city centre

Geography has affected the region in a variety of ways. The sierras and Alpujarras remain largely unscarred by major road networks (the one high pass road connecting the Alpujarras directly with the city of Granada has actually been closed), which has benefited the environment but kept agriculture and other businesses small scale. Many of the smaller villages have been maintained by an influx of foreigners. With much of Andalucía's olive production concentrated in Jaén province to the north (said by *National Geographic* magazine to be the largest olive growing region on the planet), and much of the intensive cereal farming sited in the west around Seville, agriculture has been, if not inconsiderable, then piecemeal.

So too with culture and politics. When Córdoba and Granada faded from prominence following the Reconquest, power and business shifted west to Seville and Cádiz. Even the Alhambra, one of the great tourist destinations of the world, was still languishing in semi-decay for much of the 19th century, when literary travellers such as Richard Ford and Washington Irving actually lived in apartments within the complex. It has been extensively renovated in the intervening century and a half, and work continues today (expect parts to be closed, especially around winter time) to keep the site from crumbling beneath the thunder of tourists' shoes.

Both capital and region remain the most recognisably Moorish parts of Andalucía, from their architecture to cuisine, and art to *costumbrismo* (customs). The city and environs also remain one of the centres of *gitano* (gypsy) culture in Spain, romanticised by the likes of Ford in the 19th century, and, some would say, vilified in the 20th century by association with petty crime and drugs. Granada's *gitano* population remains a fount of much flamenco music and dance (although, as elsewhere, you will be hard put to find the real thing).

Yet despite the sometimes oppressive sense of history hanging over them, both city and region are also embracing the future. Although it is barely half the size of Seville, Granada has a vibrant university and youth culture, and a particularly energetic music scene, both traditional and modern. Its literary culture, which produced the likes of Federico García Lorca (*see pp124–5*) and Luis Cernuda, has no match in any comparable Andalucían city. This thirst for culture extends to jazz, film, theatre and dance festivals throughout the year.

The city centre seen from the heights of the Alhambra complex

# Granada

Dominated by the sprawling Alhambra and with a wealth of other Moorish monuments within easy walking distance of the Alhambra hill, Granada is an ideal city for strollers. It's barely one-third the size of Seville, with a similar population ratio, but has a culture to rival that of its larger sibling.

Granada glimpsed from the Palacios

The Alhambra (*see pp118–21*) is probably the single most visited tourist attraction in the whole of Spain, and even with the luxury of time on your hands in the city it is still best to arrive prepared. Queues and crowds in mid- and high-season can be considerable, and there is a strict limit on the number of visitors allowed per day as well as a staggered entry system to the star attraction, the Palacios Nazaries. Go early in the day and early in your visit, as you may want to return after visiting its neighbours such as the Albaicín.

## Albaicín

This 'dormitory' suburb to the palace and fort on the hill is roughly contemporary to the Alhambra, and was originally a centre of mosques, palaces and gardens. Nowadays it is home to various Moorish and post-Reconquest monuments, including the 11th-century Arab baths, the Catholic Kings' Chancery and the Archaeological Museum. Best approached from Plaza Nueva or the Gran Via de Colón, it is a warren of largely pedestrian alleys, and ideal for a leisurely walk (*see pp122–3*).

Bag snatches are an occasional hazard, here and elsewhere, and you should exercise caution after dark.

## Catedral and Capilla Real

Granada's mountainous cathedral, begun by Diego de Siloé in the 16th century but only completed in the 18th is, despite its size, decidedly modest in its interior. Light and airy, thanks to its 27m (88.5ft) high dome, its various chapels feature sculptures by Alonso Cano and an El Greco portrait of St Francis.

Of greater interest is its neighbouring Capilla Real, built as a mausoleum for the *reyes catolicos*, Isabel and Fernando, as well as their daughter Joana, 'el loco' (mad) and her husband Felipe, 'el guapo' (handsome). There is, however, doubt whether these are the true remains of Isabel and Fernando, as their original graves in the Alhambra had been defiled before the contents were moved to the Capilla.
*Gran Vía de Colón Catedral and Capilla Real both open: daily, Apr–Sept 10.30am–1pm & 4–7pm; Oct–Mar 10.30am–1pm & 3.30–6.30pm. Admission charge.*

### Plaza Bib-Rambla

A few short blocks from the corner of Gran Via and Reyes Catolicos, south of Plaza Nueva, this is the nearest this oddly de-centred city has to a centre. The pretty square is lined with bars and restaurants, handy for the cathedral and, off its northeast corner, the Centro José Guerrero, a cool modern art gallery dedicated to the works of Granadino artist Guerrero, a contemporary of Pollock and Rothko, and also opening its spaces to younger Spanish artists.

*Centro José Guerrero, calle Oficios. Open: Tue–Sun 11am–2pm & 5–9pm. Free.*

### Nightlife

Here and around Plaza Nueva and the lower reaches of the Albaicín are the best places to hunt for a meal, drink or entertainment. The large student population and a lively lesbian/gay community guarantees a plethora of trendy hangouts in the lower Albaicín and environs.

The red fort in winter with the snows of the Sierra Nevada in the distance

More perhaps that any other historic monument in Spain, the Alhambra repays a little pre-planning before a visit. Such is the pressure of tourism on the site that a special system has been set up to process advance ticket applications for the 8,800 visitors allowed in each day. Some 75 per cent of tickets are available through the Banco Bilbao Vizcaya (BBV) by credit card purchase and the rest are sold at the Alhambra itself. Tickets can be purchased by credit card in advance by telephone (*902 22 44 60; from abroad: 00 34 91 346 59 36*) or via the Alhambra's website (*www.alhambra-patronato.es*), which has information in Spanish and English as well as a sister site, *www.alhambra tickets.com*, for online ticket purchase.

## Access

The Alhambra is reached from Plaza Nueva by car, the special Alhambra

bus service or on foot (*20 mins*) up the steep wooded Cuesta (hill) de Gomérez. There's a large car park by the entrance, which is to your left.

## Planning your Visit

The authorities reckon the average visitor needs three hours to visit the Alhambra, which is a conservative estimate. The Alhambra currently opens at 8.30am (ticket office: 8am) and whatever time you decide to visit your ticket will be stamped with a half-hour window (usually an hour or more in advance) during which you must enter the Palacios Nazaries area, although once past the entrance you can stay as long as you like. You should thus plan your route through the Alhambra around this. There are toilets and refreshments (sometimes just vending machines) at various points around the complex, and you should bear in mind that much of the site is out in the open (take hats and sunblock). There is wheelchair access, but not to every nook and cranny, and parts can be very crowded.

A final word of warning: some guidebooks recommend taking a picnic, a lovely idea but alas also the fastest and most ignominious route out of the Alhambra. Regulations about food and other forbidden activities are strict: in theory, making noise or being impolite to an attendant are enough to get you ejected.

## History

The oldest parts of the Alhambra, notably the Alcazaba (fortress), date from the 9th century, and later additions up to the 14th century. Ownership changed abruptly after the long winter of 1491–2, when Isabel and Fernando with an army of 150,000 laid siege to this last bastion of Moorish rule, defeating Boabdil in January 1492.

The Alhambra takes its name from the Arabic *Al Qal'a al-Hamra* (red fort), from the red-coloured walls of its earliest structures. Little of the earliest fortress remains, and it was rebuilt in the 11th century and again in the 13th by the Nasrid rulers who were to build the Palacios Nazaries.

The Alcazaba is one of three groups of monuments here, along with the Casas Reales, which include the Palacios, and the adjoining Generalife gardens.

At its peak in the 14th century, the Alhambra comprised an entire royal city in miniature.

## Alcazaba

Much of the original fort is ruined, but some vestiges remain, most notably the **Torre de la Vela** belltower, named after the bell that used to be rung to mark the hours of the irrigation system that watered Granada's Vega, or agricultural plain. The Christian flag was first flown from this battlement on 2 January 1492 to announce the city's capture.

## Palacios Nazaries

Across the **Plaza de los Aljibes** (Cisterns) is the entry to the Palacios,

Facing page: The Alhambra's masterpiece, the Patio de los Leones
Above: The Palacio del Partal, the oldest remnant of the fort

down a ramp or stairs. This is the area of the Alhambra where you will be allotted a half-hour window to enter – miss it and you'll have to come back another day or buy another ticket. The Palacios are all built around water, light and open spaces. Traffic through them, especially if you get caught between the combat-ready hordes that roam the complex led by their commando-like guides, is slow and one-way.

## Mexuar

The first section of the Palacios is a council chamber built around a courtyard in 1365 where the sultan would consult with his viziers and also hear petitions for mercy or favour from his subjects. It leads on through the **Patio del Cuarto Dorado** (Gold Quarter) to the first of the Palacios' marvels, the Serrallo, or harem.

Below: The exquisite Patio de la Acequia in the Generalife gardens

## Serrallo

The palace that housed the sultan's wives is approached through the cool (if, these days, somewhat overcrowded) rectangular space of the **Patio de Arrayanes**, named after the trimmed myrtles that hedge its placid pond. As well as the rooms giving on to the arcaded spaces around the pool, this is dominated by the **Salón de Embajadores** (Hall of the Ambassadors), where sensitive matters of state were dealt with and where Boabdil negotiated his surrender in 1492. The Salón has a magnificent latticed wood ceiling, whose criss-crossed knot-like patterns represent the seven heavens of Moorish cosmology.

## Harén

The centre of the Serrallo, where the *harén* (harem) occupants would recline, is also the archetypal feature of the Alhambra: the **Patio de los Leones**, with its twelve lions supporting a fountain at the centre of symmetrical water courses, overlooked by delicate Mudéjar arcading.

The neighbouring **Sala de los Abencerrajes**, named after the family of a rival of Boabdil slaughtered at a banquet here, has the most impressive ceiling of the entire Alhambra. Its fantastical stucco patterns are based on Pythagoras' famed theorem about the properties of the right-angled triangle.

## Palacio de Carlos V

The exit from the Palacios leads into this later, Christian addition to the complex, built in the 16th century by the eponymous king. This Renaissance palace was never finished, but now serves as the **Museo Hispano–Musulman** (*open: Tue–Sat 9.30am–2pm; admission charge, EU citizens free*) which has an excellent collection of Spanish–Moorish artefacts.

## Convento de San Francisco

Behind the palacio are the remains of the original royal city, including its convent, nowadays serving as Granada's over-priced *parador* hotel, which is often booked up months in advance. The bar and restaurant are open to non-residents, and the garden is a great place to drink in the view.

## Generalife

The neighbouring gardens, translated variously from the Arabic *Yannat al Arif* as 'gardens of the architect' or 'lofty paradise', were begun in the 13th century and originally included orchards and pasture. Later designs transformed them into a maze of exquisite water courses and topiary ideal for romantic intrigues (and, if you're really careful, a sneak baggie picnic).

**Alhambra and Generalife** (*open: May–Oct 8.30am–10pm, Nov–Feb 8.30am–6pm*).

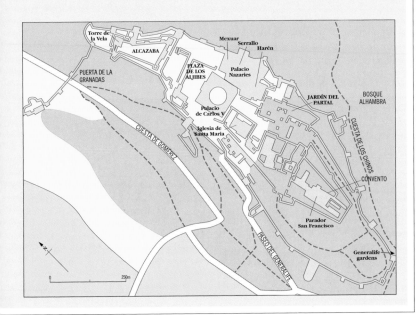

# Walk: Moorish Granada

This is a very different walk from the others included so far: urban, concerned chiefly with architecture and history, comfortably short, convenient for bars and restaurants, with numerous shopping opportunities, and with an easy duration from around one hour to as long as you care to extend it. With the exception of the walk in Córdoba (*see pp144–5*), this is one of the best opportunities to experience Moorish Andalucía: Granada's Albaicín district is interspersed with Mudéjar and later architectural styles.

### 1 Plaza Santa Ana (Plaza Nueva)
The walk begins at the Plaza Nueva in front of the rather impressive Real Chancilleria, the royal chancery of the *reyes católicos*, designed by Diego de Siloé and completed in 1530. It is now a courthouse, but you should also be able to glimpse the interior courtyard, also by de Siloé. Diagonally across on the Plaza Santa Ana is the Iglesia de Santa Ana.

### 2 Calle San Juan de Los Reyes
The walk takes a right behind the Chancilleria. Along calle Aire, the route turns on to one of the Albaicín's main thoroughfares, calle San Juan de Los Reyes, and heads east up into the Albaicín.

### 3 Iglesia and Mirador de San Nicolas
At Plaza Concepción take the left fork, heading for Plaza Trillo, which leads on

The Real Chancilleria, royal chancery, built for the *reyes católicos* by master architect Diego de Siloé

to the Iglesia and Mirador de San Nicolas, where church and *mirador* (viewpoint) have spectacular views over the Alhambra (which actually recommends you visit for the view).

### 4 Riverside Walk

From here you can either head further along Cuesta Cabras to Cuesta de Chapiz and right towards the river Darro, or back down to Plaza Trillo, left on to calle Limon and right on to calle Zafra, which will also take you to the river. Here, the carrera del Darro follows the rio Darro down towards the city centre, where the river disappears under a vast 20th-century urban development. The river was actually diverted here in the 11th

century from its natural course 8km (5 miles) away on the order of Nasrid ruler ibn al-Ahmar, to irrigate the Alhambra and its gardens. Bars and cafés line the route, overlooking the Alhambra.

### 5 Convento de Santa Catalina

Where calle Zafra turns into the Carrera del Darro sits the 16th-century Convento de Santa Catalina, where most days of the year (except August) the nuns sell their convent *dulces* (sweet cakes) through a *turno* (screen). Next to it is the Museo Arqueológico (*open: Tue 3–8pm, Wed–Sat 9.30am–8pm, Sun 9.30am–3pm; admission charge, EU citizens free*), with an excellent collection ranging from palaeolithic (around 30,000 BC) up to Moorish times.

### 6 El Bañuelo

Two blocks down are the magnificent 11th-century Moorish baths of El Bañuelo, whose vaulted interiors are illuminated by typical star-shaped ceiling apertures. (*Open: Tue–Sat 10am–2pm; free. El Bañuelo has been undergoing renovation but is expected to reopen shortly.*) From here, the picturesque riverside route back down the Carrera del Darro from the Albaicín continues down to the Plaza Santa Ana and passes the Iglesia Santa Ana, a 16th-century Mudéjar church, although the tower is in fact the minaret of an earlier Moorish mosque over which the church was built.

This route can be used to explore further into the Albaicín, whose shops specialise in Moroccan as well as local arts and crafts. For some high-class shopping, head further west, into the pedestrian precincts around Plaza Bib-Rambla, Granada's shopping heart.

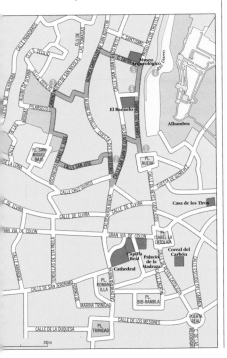

# Around Granada

Although the immediate surroundings of Granada are mostly indifferent, there are some remarkable sights within a short journey west, and a famous poet's youthful haunts are a mere bus ride away.

Guadix cave dwelling

## Guadix

One of the most remarkable urban sights in the whole of Andalucía, visible by bus, car or train from Granada, is the lumpy sandstone landscape around Guadix. The hills first appear at neighbouring Purullena, as do the tell-tale television aerials jutting from the ground. In Purullena, like its neighbour, many people live underground (an estimated 10,000 of them in Guadix), in modernised cave dwelling believed to have been in use since Paleolithic times.

The cave district of Guadix is an easy walk or drive signposted from the centre, which also boasts an impressive

sandstone cathedral by de Siloé and an attractive *casco antiguo*. There's a good museum at the heart of the district. A new luxury hotel on the edge of town also offers cave accommodation.
*Cueva Museo, Plaza Padre Podreva, Guadix. Open: Mon–Sat 9am–2pm & 5–7pm. Admission charge.*
*Hotel Pedro Antonio Alarcón, avenida de Buenos Aires, Guadix. Tel: 958 66 49 86.*

## The Lorca Trail

A short journey west of Granada brings you to three key sites in the brief life of Spain's greatest poet of the 20th century, Federico García Lorca. His *casa natal* (birth house), in Fuente Vaqueros, is the most rewarding. *Aficionados* may want to pursue the trail east to Viznar, where Lorca was assassinated.

### Fuente Vaqueros

Fuente Vaqueros is an unremarkable little town, but the tiny Museo-Casa Natal signposted near the town centre has preserved Lorca's childhood home and its contents.
*Museo-Casa Natal Federico García Lorca, calle Poeta García Lorca. Open: daily, Apr–June 10am–1pm & 4–6pm, July–Aug 10am–2pm, Sept–Mar 10am–2pm & 5–6pm. Admission charge. Tours are hourly.*

Federico García Lorca's *casa natal* in Fuente Vaqueros

## Huerta de San Vicente

The *huerta* (market garden) that the
Lorca family moved to outside Granada
has also been opened as a museum, and
is planned as the centre of a belated
memorial garden in Lorca's name.
*Calle de la Virgin Blanca, Granada
(Bus 4 from Gran Via). Open: Tue–Sun
10am–1pm & 5–8pm. Admission charge
(free Wed; EU citizens free).*

## Valderrubio

The house where Lorca's family moved
when he was six, staying only a few years
before moving into Granada itself, has
also now opened as a museum.
*C/Iglesia 34, 958 45 44 66.*

## Viznar

The town on whose outskirts Lorca
was killed by fascists has also opened
a park in his memory. The poet was
targeted during a general round-up
of Republicans and shot along with
two others in an olive grove outside
the town.
*Parque Federico García Lorca, Viznar.
On A-92 10km (6.2 miles) from Granada.*

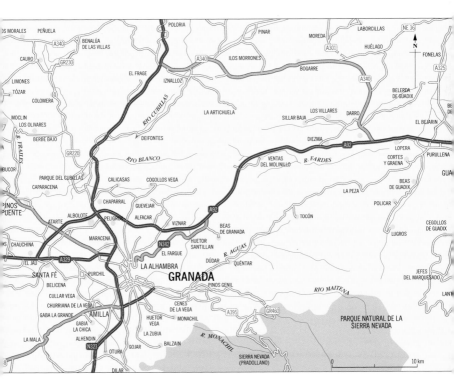

# Sierra Nevada: Skiing at Pradollano

Just 31km (19.25 miles) and 45 minutes' drive southeast of Granada is Pradollano, Europe's southernmost ski resort, with a season running from late November until the end of February. It has staged various winter sports tournaments, is a major snowboarding centre and also boasts that it has the most sunshine of any European ski resort.

Pradollano transport

Also known as Solynieve (sun and snow) and, confusingly, Sierra Nevada, it has over 50 different marked runs in seven different areas of the mountain, at altitudes roughly between 2,000m (6,561ft) and 3,000m (9,842ft) above sea level. These range from easy to very difficult, but also include training slopes and areas dedicated to non-skiing pastimes including snowbiking, sledding, luge and tobogganing.

There is also a wide range of accommodation, ranging from youth hostels to smart four star hotels, as well as restaurants, bars, banks, boutiques and even a cinema. Most of these open for the short-lived November–February ski season, although some restaurants, bars and shops (but not hotels) open to serve summer trade, as well as during the run-up to and close-down at either end of the season. The Granadinos who have made it so popular tend to head straight for the piste, and it should be pointed out that Solynieve is no Gstaadt: its bars, cafes and boutiques might more accurately be compared with a large motorway services station.

Ecologists take a dim view of the resort, particularly in such an area as the Sierra Nevada, although the resort claims to be pursuing an ecologically sensitive policy. The impact of thousands of visitors a day, however, intent on skiing to the extent that the resort has one of the largest high-tech snow-making systems in Europe, deploying hundreds of 'cannons' and 'guns' to fire instant piste on to the slopes, has to be considerable.

Non-skiers and sightseers are allowed on to three of the transport systems around the slopes, the Parador chairlift and the Al-Andalus and Borreguiles cable-cars, which include round-trip rides up to the higher slopes. The ski station (Estacion Esqui) itself, where dozens of *taquillas* (ticket windows) open to deal with the hordes who descend when ski conditions are good, also rents out a complete range of clothing and gear, as do some hotels (including the youth hostel). Equally, however, the resort welcomes those who just want to lark about on dustbin-lid style plastic sleds. There are also routes

for dog-sledding and horse-drawn sleighs, snowmobiling and inflatable toboggans. Away from the slopes, there is also an astronomy programme and there are hiking routes around the resort.

There are four daily buses from Granada to Pradollano (five at weekends), leaving from one of the stops on the roundabout by the Palacio de Congresos (over the rio Genil from downtown central Granada). There is also a twice-daily out-of-season service, as well as possible alternatives from the main bus station on the western limits of the city, situated near the *circunvalación* (bypass). Call the ski station's interactive phone line for further details (*tel: 958 24 91 19*).

Thousands of Granadinos take to the slopes on winter weekends

# Walk: Sierra Nevada/ Pradollano

This is one of the shorter mountain walks, best attempted during summer months, and with optional detours or cut-offs along the way. It is circular, with an average round-trip time of five hours, less if you opt for some of the swifter return routes. It shifts between paths, track and roads. At this altitude (above 2,000m/6,561ft, rising to over 3,000m/ 9,842ft) the usual warnings about wearing firm footwear and protective clothing and taking adequate supplies and sunburn precautions need to be stressed.

The walk can be begun either from Pradollano, which has public transport connections all year round, or in the vicinity of the Albergue Universitario, the youth hostel used by students from Granada and elsewhere during study trips. This has a bus connection during summer and the winter ski season.

Heading up above the snow line

## 1 Pradollano

There are two options from Pradollano to Borreguiles, either the conventional walk described below or a quicker cheat's walk using the ski lift (not operating in summer). The second route is also an option if you just want to walk part of the way, say to the astronomical observatory, and turn back.

## 2 Albergue Universitario

If you decide to walk, take the A-395 mountain road from Pradollano up to the Albergue. Here take the path signposted off to the right heading for the Virgin de las Nieves area, one of the numerous parascending (*parapente*) spots here. This leads to the Cruce (crossroads) de Borreguiles, where the path forks left and right, the former following the road on up.

## 3 Borreguiles

The right-hand path strikes off into open country and towards the Estacion de Borreguiles ski lift station. Above the station to the west (left) is the IRAM radio telescope station, one of three observatories this route passes.

## 4 Embalse de las Yeguas

From the Estacion, the route continues up in a fairly straightforward fashion until reaching the second observatory, above a T-junction where another path joins this route from the west (your right). Continue straight on until you reach the Embalse de las Yeguas, a small lake-like reservoir, and a series of smaller lakelets beyond.

*Here another T-junction leads left and right: take the left fork, heading back towards the road at Carihuela.*

## 5 Carihuela

At Carihuela, there are various options. You are within striking distance of the peak of El Veleta, second only in height to its neighbour, Mulhacen, Spain's highest peak. Several other high-ridge walks leave here, including a circular route via Garro del Caballo, and an even longer march over the peaks to Capileira. However, these are beyond the reach of the day walker, and anyone without serious gear and experience.

*The simplest route back to Pradollano or the Albergue is by the (blocked) road as it zigzags back down, or the quicker but rougher route as the track cuts across the meanders of the road down to Cruce de Borreguiles. The path continues to shortcut across the road's turns, passing under the third observatory seen on this route, down to the Albergue.*

*A shorter winter option still is to make the walk circular but with Estacion de Borreguiles as the destination, either by taking the road and path up and the ski lift down, or vice versa.*

# Cazorla

Clinging to a mountainside in the sierra named after it, the high mountain town of Cazorla could almost be Alpine, with its jumble of gable-roofed houses and ski-slope-steep streets and alleys. It is also a perfect example of the endlessly varied Andalucían landscape: until you reach the treeline, the entire region is a sea of olive groves.

Cazorla and its castles

Cazorla is a year-round centre for walkers in the Parque Natural de Cazorla and its neighbour, the Segura Parque Natural, one sierra east. Cazorla is the main centre of communications, including public transport, in the area, and with the widest choice of accommodation, including, outside deepest winter, a modern *parador* some 25km (15.5 miles) into the park. It is also a convenient launching-off point for those in search of the source of the Guadalquivir river, which wells up beneath boulders in a mountain crevasse south of the town before beginning its 700km (435 miles) journey across Andalucía to the sea at Sanlúcar.

## What to See

Although it is nearly 1,000m (3,280ft) above sea level, Cazorla has been an important base in the region since Roman times, and its two ruined Moorish castles, one in the centre and the other on the outskirts, record its prominence during the centuries before the Reconquest. (In fact, the Moors took their architecture even higher into the mountains – see pp132–3.)

**Iglesia Santa María**
Cazorla has one of the most dramatic churches in the region: the 16th-century church of Santa María, razed by Napoleon's troops, overlooks a gorgeous square that shares its name.
*Plaza de Santa María.*

**La Yedra**
The castellated remnant that now houses Cazorla's folklore museum, this is one of the remaining parts of the two Moorish castles (both ruins) that overlooked the town.
*Museo de Artes y Costumbres, La Yedra, Plaza de Santa María. Open: Mon–Sat 9.30am–2pm. Free.*

**Getting Around**
Apart from the elegant *palacio* housing the *ayuntamiento* (council) in the neighbouring Plaza de la Constitución, there is little else to see in Cazorla, apart from the innumerable views out over the olive-covered hills. In fact, most people visiting Cazorla spend much of their time leaving it, either into the hills on foot or by jeep or horse on treks organised by travel companies such as Quercus. There are also two official

tourist information offices here, both off Constitución, with free maps, fliers and other information.

While its hotels sport outdoor swimming pools and there are several campsites on the outskirts of town, on either side of the summer months Cazorla also gets its fair share of bad weather, which can make even the lower road routes impassable to cars without chains on their wheels. This can also increase hazards for those exploring the park on foot: rarely a winter cold spell passes without walkers being lost in the Parque Natural. The gentle undulating landscape can be deceptive, as can those heat-loving olive trees: when it snows, thousands of *olea Europea* disappear under feet of it.

*Quercus, Plaza de la Constitución. Tel: 953 72 01 15. Open: Mon–Sat 9am–2pm & 6–9pm.*

The ruins of the Iglesia Santa María at the centre of Cazorla

# Walk: Parque Natural de Cazorla

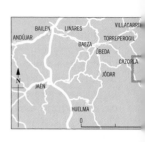

Both in summer and winter, the mountain routes above Cazorla offer some of the most spectacular views in the whole of Andalucía. This route, largely on roads, involves some improvisation with transport, or some serious hiking, but the vistas are worth it. There are numerous off-road routes around Cazorla, best taken with the guidance of one of the travel companies in the town, but they require at least a two-day stay in Cazorla.

*This route can be completed in half a day, although you might want to factor a local cab ride into part(s) of the route. Allow about 4 hours.*

### 1 Quesada

*The route actually begins in Cazorla's sister village of Quesada, although it could be begun by taking the mountain road opposite the oil station on the A-319 on the Úbeda road just outside Cazorla.*

Olive groves between Cazorla and Quesada

Quesada itself is a small mountain village with little tourism, although it has an intriguing museum to local painter Rafael Zabaleta, who reappears later on this route.

### 2 Puerto de Tiscar

The road south towards Tiscar rises into the mountains below spectacular cliffs to the east (your right). Views in the opposite direction are out over the Sierra de Cazorla and the sea of olive groves below, and just get better and better. The little-used road (a particular favourite of locals) winds up through pines to the plateau of the Puerto de Tiscar, the Tiscar Pass. At 1,800m (5,940ft), this is only 200m (660ft) below the peak of Cabañas, the elephantine mountain looming over Cazorla. Views back, and, shortly, forwards, are stunning, perfected only if you climb up to the Moorish *atalaya* (watch tower), a short clamber up from the road.

### 3 Tiscar

From here the road begins to wind down towards the hamlet of Tiscar, below increasingly dramatic rock cliffs and overhangs, and, as often as not, raptors circling on thermals. As Tiscar comes into view below, so does a distinctly architectural shape in the jagged rock formations silhouetted above it. This is the Santuario de Tiscar, a Moorish fort built on a dizzying perch above the gorge carrying the rio Quesada. The fort was captured by the Christians in the early 14th century and turned into a shrine to the Virgin Mary. Today it boasts a painting by Zabaleta recording Quesada's annual *romeria* (religious procession) to the Virgin here.

*There are a number of restaurants here, overlooking the river, where you might stop for lunch or arrange for a Cazorla cab to collect you.*

### 4 Huesa and Cabañas

A right-hand turning just beyond Tiscar leads down to Huesa and a lower route returning to Quesada. Alternatively, the same road on from Tiscar continues up on to the flank of Cabañas, past an extensive fire-damaged area of forest, and to a turning off that will lead, at some distance, to the source of the Guadalquivir, a journey only really viable by four-wheel drive. Beyond the turning for Hinojares, the road drops swiftly towards the uninteresting village of Pozo Alcón, where the landscape flattens out into the high mountain pastures east of Granada. The Guadalquivir turning – Nacio de Guadalquivir – is where the interesting landscapes peter out. The views alone would repay simply retracing your steps from here.

# Úbeda & Baeza

Úbeda is an exquisite Renaissance gem, its smaller neighbour Baeza only slightly less so. Neither has any major monuments of note, but indifferent suburbs conceal almost perfectly preserved historic centres where the visitor can step back centuries.

Úbeda's Plaza Vázquez de Molina

Both Úbeda and Baeza trace their histories back to the Roman presence, but the towns we see today were created after the Reconquest, when both fell to the Christians within a short time of each other in the 13th century. Each was built by the newly landed gentry created by the *reyes católicos*, although this process was not without its tensions. Inter-clan rivalries in Úbeda grew so fierce that the royal family had the town walls demolished so that the army could intervene in the battles raging between its dynasties (after whom most of the streets and edifices are named today).

## Baeza

Baeza too had its awkward customers: Isabel ordered that its Alcázar be torn down because sparring families kept using it as a redoubt in their violent squabbles. The Renaissance marvels that remain intact are a short stroll from the central Plaza de España and Paseo de la Constitución. Just off the southern tip of España is Baeza's most striking Renaissance palace, the **Palacio de Jabalquinto**, and next to it the **Antigua Universidad** (Old University). Nearby is the town's cathedral, **Catedral de Santa María**, with a nave by Vandelvira.

*Palacio de Jabalquinto, calle Romanones (patio only). Open: Tue–Sun 10am–1pm & 4–6pm. Free.*
*Catedral de Santa María, Plaza de Santa María. Open: daily 10.30am–1pm & 4.15–6pm. Free.*

### Ayuntamiento

Originally the town court and prison, this remarkable building of 1559 sits a block from Paseo de la Constitución on calle Benavides; parts of it are open to the public. On the corner is the (private) house occupied by a former Antigua Universidad employee, the poet Antonio Machado, who also has a *paseo* named after him on the eastern edge of the town. The greatest concentration of Renaissance palaces is to be found north of here.

*Ayuntamiento, calle Benavides. Open: Mon–Fri 9am–2pm. Free.*

### Úbeda

Despite a worrying preponderance of illiterate fascist graffiti in its new town, the old centre of Úbeda is so postcard-perfect it could be a film set. Between Plaza de Andalucía and the southerly town walls near Puerta de Granada, magnificent palaces and mansions jostle for attention along its cobbled streets and squares. At its heart sits the Plaza Vázquez de Molina, named after one of the aforementioned feuding families. This one square boasts no fewer than five buildings by Renaissance master Andrés de Vandelvira. On the west side is the **Palacio de las Cadenas**, which now houses the *ayuntamiento* and a small **Museo de Alfarería**, dedicated to Úbeda's historic ceramics trade. At its eastern end is the fantastical Gothic church of **Santa María de los Reales Alcázares**, the neighbouring **Carcel del Obispo**, and across from this the **Palacio de Marqués de Mancera**, which faces the **Palacio del Condestable Dávalos**, nowadays Úbeda's *parador*. There are more Vandelvira buildings to be found in the neighbouring Plaza del Primero de Mayo and nearby streets. The remaining city walls encircling the *casco antiguo* can be circumnavigated in under an hour.

*Museo de Alfarería, Plaza Vázquez de Molina. Open: daily 10.30am–2pm & 5–7pm. Free.*

*Santa María de los Reales Alcázares, Plaza Vázquez de Molina. Open: daily 10am–2pm & 5–7.30pm. Admission charge.*

Baeza's Plaza Santa María

# Jaén

Probably the least prepossessing city in Andalucía, Jaén nevertheless has a number of attractions worth a detour and makes an excellent base or overnight stop for exploring the region. Its Santa Catalina castle (best viewed at twilight arriving from Granada) has one of the most dramatic sites in the whole of Spain.

The Baños Árabes

A centre of olive production since Roman times and earlier (archaeological finds have established links with Greek sea traders), Jaén city and province have been dominated, geographically and economically, by the doughty *olea Europea* for millennia (and at the expense of more profitable employment). A key post in Moorish Al-andalus, it was recaptured by Fernando III's armies in 1246 and entered an economic decline that only saw an upswing in the past century. Modern-thinking authorities have been busy renovating many of Jaén's monuments and have declared free entry to and for all.

The spectacular castle (**Castillo de Santa Catalina**) is now a draughty and camply cod-baronial *parador* (*bar/restaurant open to non-guests*) and at 5km (3.1 miles) by road and an hour on foot is best experienced at a distance. In the town, however, particularly in the *casco antiguo* behind the monumental cathedral, there are some fascinating sights. Jaén is also a university town, with a separate art school, and a student culture to match.

## Catedral

The cathedral itself dwarfs the town almost as much as the Catalina castle – its twin towers are over 60m (196ft) high. Tinkered with by a variety of architects over the centuries, including Andrés de Vandelvira, it's a masterpiece of Renaissance architecture. The cathedral museum holds some important religious artefacts collected from around the region.
*Catedral, Plaza de la Constitución/Santa María. Open: daily 8.30am–1pm & 5–8pm. Cathedral museum open: Sat & Sun 11am–1pm. Free.*

## Baños Árabes

Probably the most important site after castle and cathedral is the Arab baths, among the finest preserved examples in Spain, and in fact just one of three museums now housed in a 16th-century palace that was deliberately built over the remains.

The baths themselves, built on what were probably the remains of earlier Roman baths, taking advantage of hot water springs that suggest volcanic activity in the region, are still being excavated. A glass floor has been placed over the central sections so that visitors walk over the remains as though through the air (a somewhat dizzying experience).

Above the baths, in the ground floor and upper levels of the 16th-century **Palacio de Villadompardo**, are an **ethnological museum** dedicated to the olive industry and domestic customs over the centuries. The ethnology museum shares its upper floor with a curious **Museo Internacional de Arte Naif**, a collection of largely Spanish naïve art. A lower gallery is also dedicated to contemporary art works. Under the free entry system, one ticket gets you into all these galleries. The palace, built around an elegant courtyard, is itself worth a visit.
*Baños Árabes, calle Martínez Molina. Open: Tue–Fri 9am–8pm, Sat–Sun 9.30am–2.30pm. Free.*

### Museo Provincial
This small museum dedicated to local history is also worth a visit for its fascinating collection of Iberian sculptures dating from around the fifth century BC and displaying a marked Greek influence, further suggesting an early Greek presence in this olive-dependent region.
*Paseo de la Estación. Open: Tue 3–8pm, Wed–Sat 9am–8pm, Sun 9am–3pm. Free.*

Jaen's mountainous cathedral looming above the old town

# Córdoba

The capital of the smallest region in Andalucía is unique among Andalucían, perhaps even Spanish, cities: a living Moorish city built around one of the greatest Moorish monuments in western Europe, la Mezquita. Córdoba's star has waned in recent years – it was overtaken by Ronda as the third most-visited Andalucían city in 2001 – but that cannot diminish its very special atmosphere.

The Mezquita interior

## History

Archaeologists have tracked agricultural settlements here back to the neolithic period (4000–2000 BC) and have found evidence of trade – possibly seaborne, with olive-tree-bearing Greeks – dating back to the second millennium BC. Córdoba, or Corduba as it was named, became an important city under Roman rule in the 2nd century BC, and from 152 BC was the capital of Rome's Hispania Ulterior, the northernmost region of Baetica (Roman Spain) and roughly the size and shape of Andalucía. The city prospered on agriculture and mining, and produced the poets Lucan (AD 39–65) and Seneca (AD 4–65), tutor and ill-fated mentor to Nero.

With Roman influence in decline, Córdoba – like the rest of the Iberian peninsula – fell prey to Visigoth and Vandal insurgence. The city was taken by the Moors in 711, the same year that Tariq ibn Ziyad landed at Gibraltar. In 756 it was declared the capital of Moorish Spain, under Abd ar-Rahman, who proclaimed himself the emir, independent ruler, of al-Andalus, and head of the Omayyad dynasty.

Ar-Rahman oversaw the building of la Mezquita between 785 and 787 – later rulers would expand and alter it (*see pp142–3*).

By 929, with Abd ar-Rahman III now self-declared caliph and wholly independent of Baghdad, Córdoba was the largest city in Europe. In effect, the concentration of knowledge, culture and power made Córdoba the centre of the western world. This high water mark in the city's history would produce such thinkers as Averroës and Maimonides (*see pp12–13*).

The Omayyad dynasty was torn apart in the 11th century by internecine battles between rival Berber tribes and insurgent Christian Reconquista armies from the north. Córdoba slipped into the shadow of Seville, and finally fell to the Christians in 1236. It then entered a period of economic and political decline that was only reversed in the latter half of the 20th century.

## The Modern City

Córdoba is a compact and walkable city, with its *casco antiguo* centred, naturally, on la Mezquita, and the later, post-

Reconquest city built around and east of the central Plaza de las Tendillas. Unusually for the larger Andalucían cities, its rail and bus termini are a short walk from the centre, which is shaped by the curving rio Guadalquivir as it passes the easterly limits of the old town.

While la Mezquita is a tourist honeytrap, perhaps unfortunately so given the level of vulgar commercialisation clustered around its walls, there is much more to Córdoba, as can be found on an easy stroll around the old town (*see pp144–5*).

## Alcázar de los Reyes Cristianos

As the name suggests, this differs from other Alcázares in that it was built by Christian, rather than Moorish, rulers. Alfonso XI had it built in 1368, and it was used by Isabel and Fernando during their campaign to conquer Granada. It was later used by the Inquisition and, later still, as a prison, until the mid-20th century. The depredations of time have erased much of the earlier detail, but it retains beautiful mosaics and other artefacts in the interior, and landscaped gardens and waterways in the grounds.

Water courses and landscaped gardens in the interior of Córdoba's Alcázar

## Plaza Santo de los Mártires

*Open: May–Sept, Tue–Sat 10am–2pm
and 6–8pm; Sun 10am–2pm; Oct–Apr,
Tue–Sat 9.30am–4pm and 4.30–6.30pm,
Sun 9.30am–3pm (gardens illuminated
May–Sept 10pm–1am).*

## Museo Arqueológico

As befits a city groaning with so much
history, Córdoba's archaeological
museum offers an excellent introduction
to its prehistoric, Roman and Moorish
past. The 16th-century mansion housing
the museum, Casa Páez, contains an
authentic Roman mosaic discovered
during renovation work.

*Plaza de Jerónimo Páez. Open: Tue
3–8pm, Wed–Sat 9am–8pm, Sun
9am–3pm. Admission charge (EU citizens
free).*

Monument to Maimonides in the Juderia

## Museo de Bellas Artes and Palacio de Viana

While many of its paintings were
siphoned off to the Prado, the Museo
still contains works by Murillo, Leal and
Zurburán. The Palacio de Viana is a
museum dedicated to the Viana family,
who began the palace in the 14th
century and whose heirs sold it in the
1980s. The guided tour is forgettable,
but the palace has no fewer than a dozen
superb patios.

*Museo de Bellas Artes, Plaza del Potro.
Open: Tue 3–8pm, Wed–Sat 9am–8pm,
Sun 9am–3pm. Admission charge (EU
citizens free).*

*Palacio de Viana, Plaza de Gome.
Open: June–Sept 9am–2pm, Oct–May
10am–1pm & 4–6pm. Admission charge.*

## Córdoba's Plazas

Córdoba's past and present meet in its
squares and plazas. Plaza del Potro was
once a livestock market and the area
maintained a fairly rough reputation
for centuries. Renovated, it is home to
the **Posada del Potro**, named in *Don
Quixote* and nowadays a contemporary
art gallery. Plaza de las Tendillas is the
centre of the modern city, but this is
also the area where you will find many
of Córdoba's historic churches, which
are usually locked outside service hours
and best visited around early evening.

## Around Cordoba: Medina Azahara

As well as declaring himself caliph,
Abd ar-Rahman III also built an entirely
new capital 7km (4.35 miles) west of the
city. At its peak, Medina Azahara was a
fantastical creation: one hall prefigured
holographics by employing crystals to

create man-made rainbows, while another used a vast pan of mercury tilted by a slave to produce lightning effects to impress the caliph's visitors. For 30 years until its perhaps inevitable destruction, ar-Rahman dedicated a third of the caliphate's annual wealth to this bizarre indulgence, named after a favourite wife, az-Zahra. Abd ar-Rahman was eventually sidelined by one of his viziers, Ibn Abi Amir, later known as Al-Mansur (the victor), but Amir's attempts to construct his own caliphate were thwarted by civil war among various factions. Medina Azahara was razed by Berber mercenaries, and only rediscovered at the beginning of the 20th century. Barely a fraction of the site has been uncovered, but a series of vestigial structures can be seen while excavations continue.

*Open: Apr–Sept Tue–Sat 10am–1.30pm & 6–8.30pm, Sun 10am–1.30pm; Oct–Mar Tue–Sat 10am–2pm & 5–6.30pm, Sun 10am–1pm. Admission charge (EU citizens free).*
*NB: Works may affect winter opening times; tel: 957 32 91 30 to confirm.*

Córdoba's Mezquita, cathedral and Puente Romano seen from across the Guadalquivir river

# Córdoba: La Mezquita

Córdoba's Mezquita (mosque) is unique in Spain, perhaps Europe: an (almost) intact 10th-century Moorish place of worship, replete with some stunning examples of Moorish architecture. Parts were later destroyed (although some time after the Reconquest) to allow the construction of a Christian cathedral, but not even this act of desecration can reduce the effect of the arch work or the exquisite *mihrab* (prayer niche).

## Construction

The Mezquita actually dates from a variety of eras, incorporating various architectural styles and materials from Visigothic and even Roman times. The building we see today was built in three distinct stages (four if we include the cathedral). The first stage, inwards from the Puerta de San Esteban and including the Patio de los Naranjos, was built in 785 by Abd ar-Rahman I, although much of his original design disappeared under the 16th-century cathedral. As would be the case elsewhere in the mosque, his architect Sidi ben Ayub incorporated materials, including the exterior wall, from an earlier Visigothic cathedral that had stood on the site.

Ayub's design was extended by Rahman I's successor Abd ar-Rahman II and again in the 10th century by Al-Hakam II, who added the grand ornamented *mihrab*. The oblong shape seen today was completed in the last years of the 10th century by Al-Mansur. His chief contribution was to extend the prayer hall to something the size of a football pitch, with an arched roof requiring 850 columns of granite, jasper and marble. Again, a great deal of this material was taken from earlier structures, including Visigothic and Roman places of worship. The Moorish arches, themselves an improvisation on an earlier Visigothic arch pattern, used alternating brick and stone to achieve the red and white motif, an innovation in Moorish architecture. While the style would later be abandoned in favour of northern European innovations, it is interesting to compare the design and visual effect of the arches and pillars with the pulsing repetitions in the arches of Antoni Gaudí.

## Catedral

The cathedral at the heart of the mosque wasn't in fact begun until 1523, following three centuries of relatively minor tinkering with the original structure. The first Christian edifice to be built within the mosque was the Capilla de Villaviciosa, built by Moorish craftsmen in 1371, followed by the Mudéjar-style Puerta del Perdón. The most serious effect of this was to wall in the prayer hall that had previously been open to the Patio de los Naranjos, where the faithful had prepared for prayer. What had been a light and airy place of worship became a dark and gloomy place of atonement.

Curiously, given the history of post-Reconquest Spain, the Córdoban authorities exercised considerable restraint in their handling of the building. It would seem that the chapter, or religious authorities, of the chapel wanted to impose a Christian edifice on the Mezquita, and in 1523 King Carlos I overruled the advice of the Córdobans and authorised the project. Famously, Carlos regretted the result of his decision, telling the cathedral architects 'You have destroyed something that was unique in the world.'

*La Mezquita. Calle Torrijos 10. Open: Apr–Sept Mon–Sat 10am–7pm, Sun 3.30–7pm; Oct–Mar Mon–Sat only 10am–5pm. Admission charge.*

The Mezquita at Córdoba is probably the most exquisite Muslim monument in the west

# Walk: Moorish Córdoba

Córdoba's old town is a particularly beautiful place for a stroll, especially during the first week of May, when the city celebrates its Feria de Patios, in which the inhabitants of the older houses decorate their patios with plants, pots, mirrors and water features.

*This short walk can be completed in under an hour. If you are visiting for the day by bus or train you can enter the old town via the Puerta de Almodóvar at the bottom of the Jardines de la Victoria and begin the walk there.*

## 1 Torre de Calahorra

The walk begins across the river at the Torre de Calahorra. Although it was built after Córdoba fell to the Christians, nowadays the tower contains a small museum dedicated to Córdoba's Moorish history and a rather portentous homily on the family of man.
*Open: 10am–2pm & 4.30–8.30pm (6pm in winter). Admission charge.*

The Mezquita tower

## 2 Calle de Torrijos

The route crosses the Puente Romano (the Moorish waterwheel on your left is a reconstruction), pausing briefly by the Puerta del Puente gate to admire the city's patron saint, San Rafael, atop his 18th-century monument. Straight ahead is calle de Torrijos, flanked on the right by the **Mezquita** (*see pp142–3*) and on the left by the **Palacio Episcopal**. The latter is now a museum of religious art (*open: Mon–Sat 9.30am–3pm; admission charge, or free with a Mezquita ticket*) and also Córdoba's tourist office.

## 3 Cardenal Herrero

Take a right by the Torre del Alminar, the site of la Mezquita's original minaret, on to Cardenal Herrero, where the modern *parador* is built on the site of a Moorish palace. At the end of Herrero, calle Blanco gives on to a number of *callejóns* (alleys), including the famous Callejón de las Flores, whose walls and courtyards erupt with flowers in spring and especially during the Feria de Patios.

## 4 Plaza Maimonides and Judería

At Calle Blanco, take Luque to Plaza Juda Levi, right on to Albucassis and up to Plaza Maimonides, where a statue of the great Moorish philosopher marks the site of his home. Here also is the small **Museo Taurino** (Bullfighting Museum; *open: Tue–Sat 8.30am–2.30pm, Sun 9.30am–3pm; admission charge*) that celebrates, among others, Córdoban legend Manolete – not to mention Islero, the bull who gored Manolete to death during a *corrida* at Linares in 1947 and whose hide is displayed by a replica of the matador's tomb. This is the heart of the Judería, the old Jewish quarter, and the site of the former **Sinagoga** (*open: Tue–Sat 10am–1.30pm & 3.30–5.30pm, Sun 10.30am–1pm; admission charge, EU citizens free*), with some fascinating Hebrew texts fashioned in Mudéjar style.

This is one of just three remaining synagogues left since the Jews were driven out of Spain after the Reconquest.

## 5 Calle Fernandez Ruano and Puerta de Almodóvar

Just beyond the synagogue, calle de los Judios leads through to the Puerta de Almodóvar, convenient if you're heading back to train or bus station. Otherwise calle de Cairuan leads down to Plaza Campo de los Martires, where there is a ruined Moorish *hammam* (bath) and the Alcázar. Beyond this is the river.

Commercialisation is fairly intense in the streets immediately around la Mezquita, although at least you can find a drink or meal here. There are also shops and bars spread around the quieter areas away from the mosque.

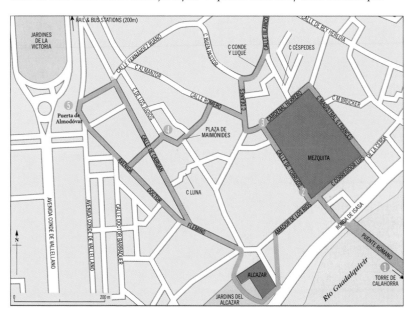

# The Reconquest

The term 'Reconquest' is a misnomer, but so in this context are the words 'Spain' and 'Moor'. Prior to Tariq ibn Ziyad's invasion of AD 711, there was no unified 'Spain' to be reconquered, rather a ragbag of small kingdoms jockeying for power, at odds with their neighbours and often found in cahoots with parts of what would later become 'France', 'Holland' or 'Germany'. Similarly, 'Moor' is a particularly wide brush used to paint numerous north African cultures.

The Reconquest was an ideological battle, as the gusto with which Isabel and Fernando pursued their agenda suggests. Having ejected the barbarians, the *reyes católicos* set about expelling Protestants, Jews, Morisco 'converts' and anyone else who disagreed with them. In modern terms, the Reconquest might be seen more as the ethnic cleansing of various peoples who had lived in Andalucía for centuries. It was also a battle to reassert vested interests: a tiny aristocratic elite became immensely wealthy by appropriating al-Andalus and the rest of Moorish Spain from the Moors.

This noted, we should also reconsider the 'Moors'. Recent decades have seen historians turning against the 'Eurocentric' reading of the Reconquest that sided with the armies of God against the armies of Mohammed. As any visitor to Seville, Granada or Córdoba will see, the Moors brought great learning to al-Andalus. A journey

through modern Andalucía will also show what their water technologies did to the near deserts here. Yet the successive waves of north African invaders were just as bellicose as their opponents, and capable of equal cruelty. The fact that it took one 'side' 709 years to win and the other 709 years to lose is surely a measure of the ferocity of the armies on both sides.

## The Element of Surprise

The Reconquest began in AD 712, perhaps when the armies of Spain had got over the shock of invasion. The real surprise was the ease with which the Berbers took the southwesternmost tip of Spain, sweeping north and meeting their first real resistance at Jerez in AD 712, where they defeated King Rodrigo and his army.

The first serious success in the Reconquest was a Christian victory at Covadonga in Asturias in AD 727, one of the few regions not to have been overrun or co-opted by the Moors. (For all their cruelty, the Moors were pragmatic about maintaining infrastructure, even allowing Christians and Jews to practise their faiths unmolested.)

For the next few hundred years or so, battlelines rippled back and forth across the Iberian landscape, frequently depositing the suffix 'de la Frontera' ('of the frontier') on spots on the map where the Christians established a foothold. The turning point came, finally, with the Christian victory at Las Navas de Tolosa, in northern Jaén, in 1212. Yet it would be another 280 years before the final Moorish stronghold, Granada, fell.

It used to be said that there were houses in Cairo, Tangier and elsewhere with the keys to houses in Granada, Ronda and other Andalucían cities still hung over the mantelpiece, waiting for their rightful owners to reclaim them from the infidels. They are, of course, already here: in the gene pool, in the architecture and, rather tellingly, in the name.

Facing page: Water wheels used to irrigate the Alcázar gardens at Córdoba
Below: Los reyes católicos, Ferdinand and Isabel, give Columbus his orders

# Beyond the resorts

From the deserted beaches of the Costa de la Luz to the ski slopes of the Sierra Nevada, and from the dune systems of Almería to the primordial forests of the Sierra de Grazalema, Andalucía boasts a variety of landscapes unrivalled in the rest of Spain. With a car or timetables for trains and buses, almost all of them are within easy reach of even the largest cities.

The only way to fly

A hire car will enable you to cross Andalucía in half a day. Public transport, however, is a good alternative, and one that will allow you to concentrate on the landscape, and people, rather than the road in front of you. It's clean, safe and efficient, although neither rail nor buses run with the frequency of northern European services. It can also be surprisingly cheap: a bus journey of a few hours or a hundred or more kilometres might cost just a handful of euros.

All but the smallest villages are served by competing private bus companies, some of which – Alsina Graells, Amarillo, Lara, Portillo – have routes that cover most of Andalucía and beyond. There are also frequent connections for destinations such as Madrid and Barcelona and destinations outside Spain as well.

Spain's excellent nationalised rail system RENFE (Red Nacional de Ferrocarriles Españoles, National Network of Spanish Trains) has a comprehensive inter-city network, which links many of the smaller towns and villages, but little in the way of suburban services (the Málaga–

Fuengirola line being a handy exception). Many services cross at the middle-of-nowhere junction of Bobadilla, equidistant between Seville and Granada, and the *enlace* (change) for trains to Málaga and Algeciras. The Ronda–Algeciras route is often listed as one of the most spectacular train rides in Europe. There are also fast links with Madrid and a daily overnight Trenhotel between Málaga and Barcelona (prices start at 68 euros). RENFE has a website in Spanish and English (*www.renfe.es*).

Andalucía also has its own modest answer to the Orient Express, the Al-Andalus Expreso. Using stylishly renovated antique rolling stock, it offers six-day itineraries around the region starting from either Seville or Madrid. Prices begin at 2500 euros (*www.alandalusexpreso.com*).

## Morocco

Most of Andalucía's coastline between Málaga and Tarifa, and inland as far as Gaucín, has views of Africa floating on its southern horizon. Algeciras, Gibraltar and Tarifa have the quickest connections to ports such as Tangier, with over 20 different ferry and catamaran services a day: most Costa del Sol resorts and towns in western Andalucía will have agencies offering day trips and longer stopovers. Both Málaga and Almería have connections with the Spanish enclaves of Ceuta and Melilla, but at six and seven hours one way this is more an extended trip and neither has the attractions of Tangier.

**Transmediterránea ferries**
*Tel: (Algeciras) 956 65 17 55; (Almería) 950 26 37 14; (Málaga) 952 06 12 18.*

## Outdoor Pursuits

Andalucía's remoter regions, notably the Alpujarras, the Serranía de Ronda and the natural parks of Cazorla and Segura, all offer a variety of outdoor activities, such as hiking, horse riding, mountain biking, canoeing, caving, climbing, canyoning, parascending (*parapente*), hang-gliding and even ballooning. Hotels and local tourist offices stock *folletos* (leaflets) about these. Travel companies such as Andalucía specialists Spain at Heart (*www.spainatheart.co.uk*) and online companies such as *www.andalucia.com* also carry this information. A number of companies also offer painting holidays in Andalucía, while others specialise in subjects including cuisine, ornithology and astronomy. Below is a selection of some of these.

## Astronomy
**Salitre Hotel and Observatorio Astronómico**
*Algatocín, Málaga;*
*www.turismosalitre.com*
Hotel-campsite in the Serranía de Ronda with its own observatory and 3.5in reflector telescope.

## Ballooning
**Glovento Sur**
*www.gloventosur.com*
Balloon flights in the Granada region (Granada city, Guadix, Sierra Nevada, Antequera and elsewhere).

## Golf
The Costa del Sol has also been officially branded and even signposted on its roads as the Costa del Golf, and has many of the region's best golf courses and associated resort hotels. The Federation de Golf de Andalucía has more than 50 courses in Andalucía, including Huelva, Cádiz, Jerez, Málaga and Almería. Its website has information in Spanish and English.

**Federation de Golf de Andalucía**
*Tel: 952 22 55 90/952 21 09 86/952 21 77 72. www.fga.org*

*Senderismo*, hiking, is the perfect way to explore Andalucía

### Horse Riding
**Dallas Love**
*Tel: 958 76 30 38.*
Horse-riding expeditions around Bubión, Alpujarras.
**El Noque**
*Ronda. Tel: 699 17 41 43.*
Horse riding through the Serranía de Ronda, with overnight stops at hotels and campsites.
**Al-hazán Rutas a Caballo**
*Tel: 956 13 22 96. www.al-hazan.com*
Day- and week-long horse trekking in the Sierra de Grazalema with multilingual guides.

The El Gato cave system outside Benaoján

### Nautical
**El Cabo a Fondo**
*Cabo de Gata. www.elcaboafondo.com*
Expeditions by semi-rigid inflatables to parts of the spectacular El Cabo de Gata peninsula, otherwise inaccessible by land.

### Skiing
For three to four months each winter, depending on regional weather patterns, **Pradollano** in the Sierra Nevada east of Granada becomes Europe's most southerly ski resort (*see p126*). Only half an hour by bus from Granada, the (rather modest) resort has over 50 slopes from nursery to black runs, skiboard runs, toboggan and sledding routes, as well as accommodation ranging from youth hostels to four-star hotels. The resort has online reservations and an interactive phone line offering weather reports and reservations.
**Sierra Nevada Club**
*Tel: 958 24 91 11.*
*www.sierranevadaski.com*

### Skydiving
**Skydivespain**
*www.skydivespain.com*
Accompanied 'tandem' parachute jumps, full, 'accelerated free fall' courses for skydiver qualification, and powered parachute flights.

### Specialist Tours
**Kirker Travel**
*Tel: (00 44) 2097 231 3333.*
Expert-led tours of the Coto de Doñana natural park.

RENFE's network of regional trains will get you from Algeciras to Jaén, and from Almería to Huelva, usually via Bobadilla

**Monte Aventura**
*Tel: 952 88 15 19. www.monteaventura.com*
Specialist in four-wheel safaris and activity pursuits in the Sierra de las Nieves.

### Walking
**Andalucían Adventures**
*www.andalucian-adventures.co.uk*
Walking holidays across Andalucía.
**Explore Worldwide**
*Tel: (00 44) 1252 760333.*
Walking in various Andalucían areas.

### Whale and Dolphin Watching
**Whale Watch**
*Paseo de la Alameda, Tarifa.*
*Tel: 956 68 47 76.*
**Foundation for Information and Research on Marine Mammals**
*calle Pedro Cortés, Tarifa. Tel: 956 62 70 08.*
Dolphin- and whale-watching safaris with two bona fide scientific

organisations (advance booking necessary).

### Indoor Pursuits
**Flamenco**
**Dance Holidays**
*Tel: (00 44) 1206 577000.*
Flamenco, salsa and tango-themed holidays in Málaga, Granada and Jerez.

### Food and Drink
**The Atelier**
*Mecina Fondales, Alpujarras;*
*Tel: 958 85 75 01. www.ivu.org/atelier*
Vegetarian and vegan hotel offering cookery courses by award-winning chef Jean-Claude Juston, author of *The New Spain: Vegan and Vegetarian Restaurants in Spain*, in this Alpujarran hamlet.
**Wine Trails**
*Tel: (00 44) 130-6 712111.*
Wine-themed tours through Andalucía.

# Shopping

Spain has joined the rest of the Eurozone states in a gradual levelling of prices in the wake of 1 January 2001 and the arrival of the euro. Like them it has also experienced a rounding up of prices – although this is not surprising when currency units changed so drastically (1000 pesetas became 600 centimos – 6 euros – overnight).

Seville street vendor

Shoes, clothes, CDs, most foods, alcohol and cigarettes remain far cheaper in Spain than in northern Europe. Books, stereos, computers and kitchen equipment are more expensive. A rising scale of IVA (*Impuesto Sobre el Valor Añadido*), more or less literally value-added tax – between 9 and 17 per cent

*Azulejos* – beautifully painted and glazed tiles

can also make a difference to prices, which are often marked up *sin IVA* (without VAT). Most tourist shops usually offer tax-free shopping.

There remain items – traditional clothing, crafts, foodstuffs such as olive oils and cured meats – that are uniquely Spanish and even uniquely Andalucían. Jaén is said to be the largest olive-growing region on the planet, and country lanes are full of signs offering virgin oil for sale. Similarly, the Atlantic Costa de la Luz is famed for its tuna, sardines and other fish, which can be found in delicatessen counters.

Seville, Granada and Marbella, and to a lesser extent Cádiz, Córdoba, Jaén, Jerez and Málaga, have shopping districts to match any northern European city. The presence of a branch of **El Corte Inglés** ('English cut'), Spain's biggest department chain, is a sign that there is serious shopping to be had, although unlike Madrid and Barcelona neither Ikea nor Habitat has arrived in Andalucía (it has its own La Oca instead). El Corte Inglés (branches: Cádiz, Córdoba, Granada, Huelva, Jaén, Marbella, Málaga, Seville) is expensive but invaluable if you need to shop for clothes, electrical goods, toiletries, medicines or international foodstuffs in a hurry. It can also stretch to furniture, musical instruments or outsized astronomical equipment.

## Books
Lavish production values make Spanish books objects of desire, although foreign language editions are rare. University cities such as Seville have at least one store with a foreign language section, notably the excellent **Vertice** opposite the university (*calle San Fernando; tel: 954 22 56 54*). El Corte usually has a selection of middlebrow English and German titles.

## Clothing
It takes immense cool to carry off wearing Spanish men's hats and even more so the *mantilla* and *peinata* (shawl and ornamental comb), but if you can they're worth the expense. *Gitano* dresses and *trajes de luces* are a no-no outside feria time.

## Crafts
The cities and countryside are excellent hunting grounds for crafts, both indigenous and imported (the Spanish are great collectors of Third World artefacts). Andalucía produces numerous forms of glazed and matt pottery, as well as its forest regions' superb (if costly) olive and oak wood products.

Andalucía's food and drink are among the most distinctive in Spain

## Food
The range of fresh and preserved foodstuffs is vast and varies enormously across Andalucía. Spain's commendable resistance to processing and factory production ensures that its food is among the finest in Europe.

## Music and Videos
New and best-selling CDs, DVDs and videos sell at similar prices to northern Europe, but back catalogues can often be a fraction of the recommended retail price, as can recordable software such as CDs and DVDs. Seville's **Sevilla Rock** on Plaza Duque de la Victoria is Andalucía's nearest equivalent to an HMV or Cologne's Saturn Records.

# Entertainment

It is barely two decades since the death of Franco and the cultural revolution known as *la movida* (the movement) that followed it. Yet in the intervening years Spain has been catching up with its European neighbours.

Flamenco *bailadora*, dancer

While *la movida* was most active in Barcelona and Madrid – perhaps led by the former's unholy offspring, film director Pedro Almodóvar, and the radical theatre group La Fura dels Baus – its impact on Andalucía's cities and towns, even conservative Granada, was notable. The Andalucían thirst for culture can be seen in the proliferating number of arts festivals, galleries and venues, and the pages of journalism dedicated to these at national, regional and local levels.

## Flamenco

When visiting Seville you are likely to encounter a personable Englishman somewhere in the city centre who will enquire whether you speak English and would like to see a flamenco show. You should decline the offer. The last way to see 'authentic' flamenco is at the invitation of an English-speaking stranger. This warning extends to the *tablaos* (flamenco shows or tableaux), promoted by hotels: at best they'll be an entertaining forgery of the real thing, at worst an extortionate rip-off. Below are some formal and informal venues likely to offer something like the real thing.

### Seville
**Asociación Antiguo Sevilla**
*Calle Castellar. Tel: 954 21 05 12.*
Cultural association with regular flamenco Wed evenings.
**Casa de la Memoria de Al-Andalus**
*Calle Ximenéz de Enciso, Santa Cruz. Tel: 954 56 06 70.*
Cultural centre dedicated to showcasing young flamenco talent. Concerts weekends and some weekdays.
**Centro Cultural El Monte**
*Calle Laraña. Tel: 954 48 48 48.*
This smart contemporary arts centre has regular seasons of first-rate new flamenco performers, such as Almería's Tomatito, as well as classical concerts.
**Sol Café Cantante**
*Calle Sol. Tel: 954 22 51 65.*
Small central café with regular flamenco (booking advised).
Bars such as **La Carboneria** (*calle Levies*), **El Mundo** (*calle Siete Revueltas*) and **El Simpecao** (*Paseo de la O, Triana*) also host flamenco performances.

### Granada
**Bar Ziryab**
*Calderería Nueva. Tel: 958 22 94 29.*
Nightly concerts of flamenco and Arabian music.

**Las Cuevas de Khayyam**
*Calderia Nueva. Tel: 958 22 68 33.*
Music, poetry and dance Thur, Fri and
Sun.
**Centro de Estudios Gitanos**
*Sacromonte.*
Regular concerts of flamenco and
related musics at this Roma cultural
centre above the Albaicín.
**Eshavira**
*Postigo de la Cuna. Tel: 958 29 08 2.*
Near-legendary Granada flamenco and
jazz club with live flamenco on Sun.

**La Guayana**
*Carrera del Darro. Tel: 660 87 44 42.*
Flamenco concerts most Sun.
Most towns across Andalucía will have
bars or organisations that host local
(and often stunning) flamenco talent.
Tourist offices, record and book stores
and some cafés will often put you on
the right trail.

**Other Concerts**
Seville's **Teatro de la Maestranza** (*Paseo de
Colón; tel: 954 22 33 44*), **Teatro Lope de
Vega** (*Avenida de María Luisa;
tel: 954 59 08 53*) and **Teatro
Central** – actually out on Isla
de la Cartuja (*calle José
Galvan; tel: 954 46 08 80*) are
its key venues for classical, jazz
and pop music. Events are
publicised around the city and
in the monthly free sheet *El
Giraldino*, a listings magazine
given away across the city.

In Granada, the **Teatro
Municipal Isabel La Católica**
(*Acera del Casino; tel: 902 15
00 25*), the **Teatro Alhambra**
(*calle Molinos; tel: 958 22 04
47; www.teatroalhambra.com*)
and the **Auditorio de Manuel
de Falla** (*Paseo de los
Martíres; tel: 958 22 21 88*)
serve the same function. The
monthly free sheet *Guía de
Granada* lists all
performances.

There are also regular
concerts in Almería, Cádiz,
Córdoba and Málaga, as well
as in smaller towns such as
Ronda and Jerez, which are

Seville's grand Teatro Lope de Vega, named after
the legendary playwright

listed in the Andalucía-wide free monthly, *¿Qué Hacer?* ('What's On?'), available in tourist offices and many hotels (also on the net at *www.andalucia.org*).

## Galleries

As well as their grand museums some Andalucían cities also have art galleries devoted to local and regional art. In Seville, both the **Museo de Arte Contemporáneo** (*Plaza de Triunfo; open: 10am–1pm; free*) and the **Centro Cultural El Monte** (*calle Laraña; open: 10am–2pm & 6–9pm; free*) stage occasional exhibitions of contemporary art. Granada's key modern art space is the **Centro José Guerrero** (*calle Oficios;*

*open: Tue–Sun 11am–2pm & 5–9pm; free*) off Plaza Bib-Rambla.
The following are also worth checking for occasional exhibitions.

### Almería
**Centro de Arte**
*Plaza Barcelona. Open: Mon–Fri 11am–2pm & 6–8pm, Sat 6–8pm, Sun 11am–2pm. Free.*
**Centro Andaluz de la Fotografía**
*Calle Conde Ofalía. Open: Mon–Fri 9am–2pm & 4–9pm. Free.*
### Jaén
**Museo Municipal**
*Calle Martínez Molina. Open: Tue–Fri 9am–8pm, Sat–Sun 9.30am–2.30pm.*

Seville's Centro Cultural El Monte has a gallery and spaces for performances and concerts by the likes of flamenco star José Merce

**Marbella**
**Museo de Grabación**
*Calle Hospital Bazán. Open: Mon–Fri
10am–2pm & 6–9pm. Admission charge.*

**Málaga**
**Casa Natal de Picasso**
*Plaza de la Merced. Open: Mon–Sat
10am–2pm & 6–8pm, Sun 10am–2pm.
Free.*
**Centro de Arte Contemporáneo**
*Calle Alemania. Open: Tue–Sun
10am–8pm. Free.*
**Museo Picasso**
*Calle San Agustin. Open: Mon–Sat*

*10am–2pm & 6–8pm, Sun 10am–2pm.
Free.*

**Ronda**
**Museo Peinado**
*Plaza del Gigante. Open: Mon–Sat
10am–2pm & 6–8pm, Sun 10am–2pm.
Free.*
**Opera & Theatre**
In Seville, the Central, Lope de Vega
and Maestranza theatres dominate the
opera and theatre scene (details as
above), and the Alhambra and Isabel
La Católica theatres (also above)
perform the same function in Granada.

Seville is the crucible of flamenco, and the Sevillana is its defining dance

The following theatres serve as chief venues for theatre and other events in towns noted for independent and touring productions.

### Córdoba
**Gran Teatro de Córdoba**
*Avenida Gran Capitán. Tel: 957 48 02 37.*

### Cádiz
**Gran Teatro Falla**
*Plaza de Falla. Tel: 956 22 08.*

### Jaén
**Auditorio Municipal de la Alameda**
*Alameda de Calvo Sotelo.*
*Tel: 953 21 91 16.*
**Teatro Darymelia**
*Calle Colón. Tel: 953 21 91 16/*
*953 21 91 80.*

### Málaga
**Teatro Cánovas**
*Plaza el Ejido. Tel: 958 22 20 22.*
**Teatro Cervantes**
*Calle Ramos Marín. Tel: 952 22 41 09.*

### Nerja
**Nerja Caves**
One of the most remarkable venues is the Nerja Cave system, which holds ballet, music and theatre performances during summer months.
*Tel: 952 52 95 20.*

### Ronda
**Teatro Espinel**
*Alameda del Tajo. Tel: 952 87 78 21.*

### Cinema
Foreign-language films are a rarity wherever you travel within Spain.

Most films are dubbed into Spanish, although occasionally a local cinema club or college arts group will present a *VO – version original –* print of a popular foreign-language film. The Junta de Andalucía's cultural division supports a touring cycle of art films twice a year, but it is unlikely that the holidaying visitor will stumble across these (although it's worth keeping an eye open).

Multiscreen cinemas are common throughout Andalucía's cities and larger towns. The fare is heavily biased to US releases, peppered with Spanish and South American productions. Even at their worst, at least they'll improve your colloquial *español.*

### Seville
**Alameda Multicines**
*Alameda de Hércules. Tel: 954 38 01 57.*
**Avenida 5 Cines**
*Marques de Paradas. Tel: 954 29 30 25.*
**Cine el Mirador**
*Avenida Kansas City. Tel: 954 57 72 20.*
**Cines Warner Lusomundo**
*Plaza de Armas. Tel: 954 91 54 32.*
These and other cinemas are also served by several websites:
*www.cinentradas.com*
*www.entradas.com*
*www.serviticket.com*
*www.warnerlusomundo.com*

### Granada
**Aliatar**
*Recogidas. Tel: 958 26 19 84.*
**Multicines Centro**
*Salarillo de Gracia. Tel: 958 25 29 96.*
**Multicines Neptuno**
*Centro Neptuno. Tel: 958 52 04 12.*

**Madrigal**
*Carrera del Genil. Tel: 958 22 43 48.*
The **Cine Club Universitario**, at
the Facultad de Ciencias, Campus
Fuenteneuva, south of the town centre,
has a regular art film programme,
listed in *Guía de Granada*. The **Teatro**

**Municipal Isabel La Católica**
also has occasional themed film
programmes.

Most local newspapers carry listings
and reviews of cinemas in Cádiz,
Córdoba, Jaén, Málaga, Marbella
and Ronda.

Summer months see the spectacular caves at Nerja hosting ballet, music and other live performances

# Children

Anyone travelling with children in Andalucía will meet a particularly warm welcome in most hotels and restaurants. Children are integrated into Spanish social life to the extent that they can often be seen out with their parents until the small hours.

Isla Magica, Andalucía's best theme park

Coastal resorts have developed various attractions aimed at younger children, including water parks, the SELWO animal park, and in Seville itself the largest theme park in Andalucía, Isla Magica. It is also worth considering trips to natural features such as the Cueva de la Pileta outside Ronda, and historic sites such as La Rabida near Huelva.

### Cueva de la Pileta
Neolithic cave system with cave art estimated at 30,000 years old, bat colony and unusual geological formations.
*On MA-561 Benaojan–Jimera de Libar (6km (3.7 miles) from Benaojan). Tel: 952 16 73 43. One-hour guided tours hourly 10am–1pm & 4–5pm. Admission charge.*

### Isla Magica
Andalucía's premier theme park with white knuckle and gentler rides, themed areas and shows.
*Isla de la Cartuja, Seville. Tel: 902 16 00 00. www.islamagica.es. Open: 11am–late. Closed: Dec–Mar (Fri–Sat only mid-Sept–Nov). Admission charge.*

### Mini Hollywood
The oldest of various Wild-West theme attractions in the Tabernas area of Almería, and the place where they shot parts of *The Magnificent Seven*, *A Fistful of Dollars*, *The Good, the Bad and the Ugly* and dozens of other spaghetti westerns. There are Wild-West extravaganzas, cancan shows and a small zoo with events throughout the day.
*On A-370 Rioja–Guadix (10km (6.2 miles) from Rioja). Open: July–Sept 10am–9pm, Oct–June 10am–7pm. Admission charge.*

### Nerja Caves
One of the largest and most commercialised of the region's cave system.
*N340 Nerja–Almunecar 4km (2.5 miles). Tel: 952 52 95 20. Open daily 10am–2pm & 4–6.30pm. Admission charge.*

### La Rabida
The key Columbus site is now a museum with historical displays and, at the *muelle* (jetty), there are life-sized models of his ships to explore.
*Monasterio de la Rábida, on N340 8km (5 miles) S of Huelva. Tel: 959 35 04 11. Monastery open: 10–11.45am &*

Granada's Parque de las Ciencias offers a hands-on intro to the sciences

*noon–6.15pm daily (closed Mon).*
*Free/donation. Muelle de las Carabellas*
*open: 10am–7pm daily (closed Mon).*
*Admission charge.*

### Parque de las Ciencias, Granada

Hands-on science park on the city
outskirts, with planetarium, science
games and various exhibitions pitched at
bloodthirsty pre-teens. The planetarium
also has viewings at its observatory
depending on sky conditions and season.
*Avenida del Mediterráneo. Tel: 958 13*
*19 00. www.parqueciencias.com. Open:*
*Tue–Sat 10am–7pm, Sun 10am–5pm.*
*Admission charge (separate charge for*
*planetarium). Observatory (included in*
*price) open until 7pm or 10.30pm (check*
*with box office).*

### Parque de Cocodriles

Said to be among the largest crocodile
parks in the world, with one beast
measuring 4m (13ft), and other wildlife
besides.
*Parque de Cocodriles, Cartáma, Málaga.*

*Tel: 952 11 83 17. Open: 10am–6pm.*
*Closed Dec–Feb. Admission charge.*

### SELWO Aventura

Andalucía's largest wildlife park, with
tours and aerial walkways through
outdoor areas where animals dwell in
habitats resembling 'natural' conditions.
*On N340 162km (103.6 miles)*
*Las Lomas Del Monte/Estepona.*
*Tel: 902 19 04 82. Open: 10am–6pm.*
*Closed Dec–Feb. Admission charge.*
*Group and other reductions including*
*Selwopack joint admission to Marina*
*and Telecabinas (see below).*

### SELWO Marina

New aquarium attraction with dolphins,
sea lions and penguins.
*Parque de la Paloma, Benalmádena.*
*Tel: 902 19 04 82. Open: 11am–7pm.*
*Admission charge.*

### Telecabinas Benalmádena

Panoramic cable-car rides into the hills
above Torremolinos, with self-guiding
walks, gardens and restaurants.
*Esplanada Tivoli, Benalmádena.*
*Tel: 902 19 04 82. Open: 10.30am–6pm.*
*Closed: Nov–Mar. Admission charge.*
*Does not run in bad weather – call for*
*confirmation.*

### Tivoli World

The largest theme park on the Costa del
Sol, with white knuckle and gentler
rides, gardens and shows.
*Avenida de Tivoli, Arroyo de la Miel,*
*Benalmádena. Tel: 952 57 70 16.*
*Open: daily 4pm–2am (weekends only*
*Oct–Nov). Closed: Dec–Mar. Admission*
*charge (children under 1m (3.3ft) free).*

# Food and Drink

Andalucía's landscape and climate have won an unrivalled reputation for the region's food and drink. Several Spanish classics originate here, and its restaurant owners have recently been making inroads into that preserve of French and more northerly establishments, the Michelin and other guides.

Taking care of Jerez's grapes

## What to Eat

It is the home of *gazpacho*, the tomato-based chilled vegetable soup, and *rabo de toro*, the oxtail stew that might be considered the consummate Andalucían *plato*. The region's fishing fleets have access to two oceans, and its vegetable growers have turned its eastern half into a giant hothouse for subtropical fruit and vegetables, and the western half into lush cereal and dairy farmland.

*Jamón*, ham, hangs air drying for at least a year

Andalucía was a late starter in the wine sector, but it has produced several whites and now a number of reds that are winning plaudits from critics. Alpujarran mountain springs produce Spain's most popular bottled water, Lanjaron, and Málaga's modest Larios distillery produces a world-class gin that many *aficionados* prefer over well-known British brands.

### Vegetarian and Vegan Foods

The situation for vegetarian and vegan eaters in Spain is improving. Most fair-sized towns have a vegetarian restaurant and many of the better restaurants will, forewarned, cater even for vegans – but sometimes vegetarian travellers have to make do with staples such as soups and omelettes. It's best to double-check vegetarian-sounding dishes, as they can sometimes be flavoured with ham or cod, or with animal stock. Many restaurateurs are used to such enquiries.

### Typical Meals and Ingredients

Specialities can vary from region to region, even village to village, but Andalucían farmers' perseverance with traditional methods produces fresh meats and vegetables wherever you eat or shop. Fish from the Atlantic and Mediterranean reaches shops and restaurants within a matter of hours. Below are some typical meals you'll encounter across Andalucía.

**Aceitunas** olives, the ubiquitous pre-meal nibble: *verde* (green) or *negro* (black), and sometimes *relleno* (stuffed), with *pimiento* (pepper) or *pepinillos* (baby gherkins).

**Aguacate** avocado, an Andalucían staple, often with *vinaigre* (vinaigrette), *con gambas* (with prawns), and occasionally but deliciously as a *sopa* (soup).

**Ajo blanco** white garlic soup, often strong; perfect hot on a cold day (and proof of food writer Katherine Whitehorn's dictum, 'If your friends don't like garlic, change your friends'), but sometimes also served cold.

**Albondigas** meatballs, often spicy, in a rich onion and herb or tomato sauce.

**Alcachofas** artichokes, sometimes with *vinaigre* (vinaigrette), *a la andaluz* (with bacon and ham), or *romana* (battered and fried).

**Almejas** clams, often *a la marinero* (in white wine and herbs).

**Almendras** almonds, found almost everywhere in Andalucía and usually served in a *postre* (dessert) such as *tarta* (flan), or sometimes as part of a *salsa* (sauce) for *pollo* (chicken).

**Alubias** beans, *blanco* (white), *verde* (green), *rojo* (red), in *estofados* (stews), *sopas*, or sometimes as *legumbres* or *verduras* (side vegetables).

**Anchoas** anchovies, a common *tapas* in vinegar, but often found in *montaditos* (small bread rolls), containing *queso* and pimiento. Also known as **boquerones**.

**Añojo** veal, commonly in *patas* (leg of), or *estofado* (stew) or with *alubias* (beans).

**Apio** celery, used in *estofados* and *sopas* or *asado* (baked), as a *verdura*.

**Atún** tuna, famously from the Costa de la Luz, often *al horno* (baked in the oven), or in the house *ensalata mixta* (mixed salad), which may be served automatically as a pre-meal taster.

**Bacalao** cod, *the* Andalucían fish dish: *a la plancha* (grilled), *frito* (fried), or with various *salsas* such as *puerro* (leek).

**Berenjenas** aubergine or eggplant, usually sliced or chipped, fried, sometimes battered and served with *miel* (honey).

**Besugo** bream, given a similar treatment to *bacalao* (cod).

**Calabacin** and **calabaza** courgette/marrow, and pumpkin, served as vegetables or a classic country *sopa*.

**Calamares** squid, often *frito*, *romano*, or *en su tinta* (cooked in its own ink).

Two oceans provide Andalucía with its definitive seafood dish, paella

**Cangrejo** crab.

**Cerdo** pork, in myriad varieties, often *de granja* (free-range).

**Champiñones** and **setas** mushrooms, a frequent *tapa*, with *ajo*, also known as *ajillo*. *Champiñones* are commonly the larger button variety, *setas* wild woodland fungi.

**Chorizo** spicy red sausages, cold and sliced as a *tapa*, cooked with *patatas fritas* (fries/chips) and often diced into *estofados*.

**Chuletas** chops, of *cordero* (lamb) or *cerdo* (pork).

**Codorniz** quail, a speciality of country restaurants – *huevos de codornices* (quail's eggs) are a delicious *tapa*, individually fried and served on bread with *jamón* (ham).

**Conejo** rabbit, commonly served as an *estofado*, with *garbanzos* (chick peas).

**Croquetas** breaded potato croquettes *relleno* (stuffed) with chicken, ham, or *espinaca* (spinach).

**Esparragos** asparagus, which grows wild all over Andalucía and is usually served steamed with *mantequilla* (butter) or *mayonesa*.

**Guisantes** green garden peas, often served as a *legumbre* with *habas* (broad beans) or *zanahoria* (carrot).

**Huevos** eggs: *duro* (hardboiled), *frito* (fried), *revuelta* (scrambled, usually with something else) or *rancheros*, in a spicy tomato sauce with *chorizo* and *alubias*.

**Lechuga** lettuce, mainstay of any *ensalata*.

**Lenguado** sole, most popular fish after *bacalao*, cooked in various ways.

**Lentejas** lentils, of various colours, used in soups or vegetable stews.

**Mariscos** seafood, but more correctly shellfish, often as a *variados* (a variety of shellfish cooked in wines and herbs), or *sopa*.

**Merluza** hake, third of the big three fish, cooked *a la plancha* or in a variety of sauces.

**Morcilla** a delicacy whose English equivalent, black pudding, can't describe what herbs, spices, breadcrumbs, pine nuts and a splash of something alcoholic can do to this robust country sausage. It's eaten sliced thin as a cold *tapa*, or hot with a *salsa*, *patatas* and *verduras*.

Seville's excellent Egaña Oriza

**Pato** duck, commonly served as *magret de* (breast of) or *a la naranja* (a l'orange).

**Pavo** turkey – as much a traditional Christmas bird in Spain as elsewhere.

**Pechuga de pollo** the most common way chicken arrives at your table: roast breast, a generous helping usually cooked in its own juices.

**Perdiz** like quail, pheasant is a popular country dish, often served with *alubias*.

**Pez espado** literally 'sword fish', customarily served as unadorned steaks, but these days an endangered species.

**Pulpo, pulpito** octopus and baby octopus, smaller and more tender than the sea monsters served in regions such as Galicia.

**Queso** cheese: not an Andalucían strong point, with *manchego* (from La Mancha) the most common, but country-made *queso de cabra* (goat's cheese) fried and topped with *confitura de frambuesas* (raspberry conserve) is a great starter and a *tapa* to be sought out.

**Rape** monkfish, also popular, and served with wine or herb sauces.

**Raya** skate, served *a la plancha* or with sauces.

**Solomillo** better-quality beef steak, served *al vino* (in red wine sauce) or simply *con patatas fritas* (steak and chips).

**Sopa** soup, a country staple and a sophisticated starter in many city restaurants. Most common is *picadillo* (bread, egg and ham), *pollo* (chicken), *pesca* (mixed fish), *verduras* (vegetable), *tomates* (tomato) and *crema de tomates* (cream of tomato). *Sopa de calabaza* (pumpkin) can be amazing (especially if tried at the lovely old former Hotel Naciónal in Gaucín), as can *sopa de tagarniñas* (wild thistle soup), which is a speciality of Grazalema and other mountain villages.

## Where to Eat

Eating out in Andalucía and the rest of Spain is not done as it is elsewhere in Europe. Andalucíans eat late: lunch from 2pm onwards is sometimes the main meal, especially at weekends. After an afternoon *merienda* or tea (around 5–6pm), dinner falls between 10pm and midnight, earlier in rural areas. Many people prefer a round of *tapas* at various bars with friends rather than a sit-down dinner. At weekends and on summer evenings, some people then think about going out for the night.

Tragabuches, Ronda's smart but friendly Michelin-starred temple to new Spanish cuisine

Marbella's excellent La Comedia, overlooking the Plaza de la Victoria

Restaurants vary considerably. Roadside *ventas*, unassuming truckers' cafés, have an excellent reputation, but some large city restaurants can be dreadful. In general, places with photographs of food should be avoided. Booking is advisable in city centre restaurants, at weekends, or if you want to eat late with the Spanish. Dress codes are rare, and might be taken as a recommendation to eat in a less pretentious locale.

The best advice is to follow the locals, eat where they eat, and leave if more than half the other diners are speaking your language.

In the following list of recommended restaurants, the price symbols indicate the approximate cost per head:

\* up to €10
\*\* up to €20
\*\*\* up to €30

## Almería
**El Alcazar** \*\*
One of the most popular bar-restaurants in the Puerta Purchena district at the heart of the old town, with a wide range of seafood *tapas* and *platos*.
*Calle Tenor Irirbarne 2. Tel: 950 23 89 95.*
**Los Mariscos** \*
Sturdy beer-and-*tapas* fish bar-restaurant, the place to eat with the locals.
*Calle Mendez Núnez 20. Tel: 950 23 54 02.*
**Mesa España** \*\*
One of the best mid-range restaurants in Almería, offering fish, meat and vegetarian alternatives.

*Calle Mendez Nuñez 19.*
*Tel: 950 27 49 28.*
**Taberna Torreluz** \*\*
A great central place for
*tapas* and drinks, and the
most informal of the
three restaurants linked
to the hotel of the same
name. No need to book.
*Plaza Flores 3. Tel: 950 23
43 99.*
**Valentin** \*\*\*
Probably the most
upmarket restaurant in
town, with an extensive
menu of delicately
prepared fish and seafood
dishes, and a complement
of meat and international
dishes.
*Tenor Iribarne 11. Tel: 950
12 44 75.*

## Arcos de la Frontera
**El Convento** \*\*
The best restaurant in
town, in an extraordinary
16th-century palace
setting. Perfect for trying
some regional specialities,
not least *perdiz en
almendras* (pheasant in
almond sauce).
*Calle Marqués de
Torresoto 7. Tel: 956 70
23 33.*

## Benaoján
**El Molino del Santo** \*\*
One of the most idyllic
restaurant settings in
Andalucía: under willow
trees by a mill stream
in the gardens of a
mountain-hideout hotel.

Offers a wide range of
local specialities using
organic ingredients,
with plenty to please
every taste.
*Estación de
Benaoján/Montejaque.
Tel: 952 16 71 51.*

## Cádiz
**1800** \*\*
A Cádiz institution, and
somewhat cheaper and
easier to book into than
El Faro, with a near
definitive *bacalao pil-pil*
(cod in garlic).
*Calle San Felix 15.
Tel: 956 21 10 68.*
**El Faro** \*−\*\*\*
Possibly the most
fabulous fish restaurant
in Andalucía, and
certainly the most fabled.
Book for the pricier
upstairs restaurant, just
roll up for the friendly
downstairs *tapas* bar, and
some wonderful
variations on fish and
seafood in either.
*Calle San Felix 15.
Tel: 956 21 10 68.*
**El Sardinero** \*
Handsomely positioned
in this small square, this
is a favourite snack and
takeout restaurant for
great fish, and the nearest
*gaditanos* get to English
takeaway fish and chips.
*Plaza san Juan de Dios 4.*

Andalucía's restaurants often have the pick of local produce

**Ventorrillo del Chato** ★★
Dating in parts from the 1780s, this is said to have been the place where *tapas* was invented, and in the 1820s was King Fernando VII's favourite restaurant.
*Playas Victoria/de Cortadura. Tel: 956 25 00 25.*

### Córdoba
**Almudaina** ★★
One of the finest of Córdoba's restaurants, and the place to try some of the most typical Córdoban dishes, *rabo de toro* (oxtail) and *salmorejo*, a thick gazpacho-like vegetable soup or stew.

Nothing can beat an al fresco tapas of jamón and a glass of chilled fino

*Plaza Camo de los Martires 1. Tel: 957 47 43 42.*
**El Caballo Rojo** ★★
The most famous restaurant in the city, specialising in local dishes dating from Moorish times, many of which still influence modern Andalucían cooking. The cheaper/quicker *tapas* bar is also recommended.
*Calle Cardenal Herrero 28. Tel: 957 47 53 75.*
**El Churrasco** ★★★
This smart restaurant completes Córdoba's trio of top-notch restaurants, and is famed for its titular pork dish, *churrasco*, in a pepper sauce.

*Calle Romero 16. Tel: 957 29 8 19.*

### Gaucín
**Hostal Naciónal** ★
Once the only hotel en route to Gibraltar, this venerable old *posada* (inn) operates occasionally as a restaurant, where the food is superb.
*Calle San Juan de Dios 8.*

### Gibraltar
**Claus on the Rock Bistro** ★★
Smart seafront restaurant with an international menu and the place where most Rock inhabitants head for a celebration.
*Queensway Quay. Tel: 48686.*
**Lord Nelson** ★
The best of the restaurants in the town's central meeting place.
*10 Casemates Square. Tel: 50009.*
**Saccarello's** ★
Popular café snack-bar, with a variety of freshly made international meals.
*57 Irish Town. Tel: 70625.*

### Granada
**Arrayanes** ★★
One of the best north African restaurants in the Albaicín, sumptuously decorated and specialising in *tagines*,

sturdy meat, fish or
vegetable stews.
*Cuesta Marañas 4.
Tel: 958 22 84 01.*
**Cuñini** **
Excellent seafood from
Andalucía and also
Galicia, this smart
restaurant off Bib-
Rambla also has a cheap
and friendly *tapas* bar.
*Plaza Pescaderia 14.
Tel: 958 25 07 77.*
**Parador de San
Francisco** **
Like its bar, a place to
splash out and enjoy
almost unrivalled views
of the Albaicín from the
garden terrace.
*Alhambra. Tel: 958 22
14 40.*
**Pilar de Toro** **
Classic *grenadino* dishes
in this elegant, converted
17th-century mansion,
which has a downstairs
*tapas* bar and upstairs
restaurant with its own
terrace.
*Plaza Nueva. Tel: 958 22
38 47.*
**Las Tinajas** **
One of Granada's
smartest restaurants,
with a mix of southern
and northern Spanish
classics, and some fine
fish dishes. Also handy
for Bib-Rambla.
*Calle Martinez Campos
17. Tel: 958 25 43 93.*

The dining room of Córdoba's venerable eaterie El Caballo Rojo

**Grazalema**
**Cadiz el Chico** **
The best restaurant in the
rainiest village in Spain,
recently remodelled
with pine, still serving
excellent food, including
a splendid *pierna de
cordero* (leg of lamb)
for two, a scorching
*sopa de ajo*, and, in
season, dishes with
*tagarniñas* (wild thistles).
*Plaza de España. Tel: 956
13 20 27.*

**Málaga**
**Antonio Martin** ***
One of Málaga's oldest
fish restaurants, and one
of the most expensive.
*Paseo Maritimo 16.
Tel: 952 22 73 98.*
**Rincon de Mata** **
Restaurant-*tapas* bar in
the centre of town with a
wide selection of classic

*Malagueño* fish and meat
dishes.
*Espartero 8. Tel: 952 21
31 35.*
**Taberna La Garrocha** **
Upmarket restaurant
offering typical *Malagueño*
dishes.
*Plaza Mitjana 2. Tel: 952
60 17 56.*

**Marbella**
**Il Cantuccio** **
Hidden in an alleyway off
calle Ancha this great
little Italian restaurant is
one of Marbella's best-
kept secrets.
*Callejón Santo Cristo 3.
Tel: 952 77 04 92.*
**La Comedia** **
Pan-global dishes – from
the Arctic circle to
Macronesia – served with
style and wit in this
trendy but friendly
designer restaurant

Andalucía has a reputation as Spain's vegetable garden

hidden in a corner of one of the *casco antiguo*'s old squares.
Booking advised.
*Plaza de la Victoria. Tel: 952 77 64 78.*

**La Tricicleta** \*\*
Opposite the Comedia, this small and intimate restaurant mixes traditional dishes with subtle variations on *nueva cocida* to great effect.
*San Lázaro s/n. Tel: 952 85 76 86.*

**Ronda**
**Pedro Romero** \*\*
Ronda's shrine to bullfighting with real bulls' heads on the walls and photographs of Hemingway and Welles hanging out with bullfighting heroes such as Antonio Ordoñez. A refit has seen the menu move somewhat upmarket, but it's still the place to try classics such as *rabo de toro*, *perdiz* and *conejo*.
*Virgen de la Paz 22. Tel: 952 87 91 14.*

**Puerta Grande** \*
This new arrival in a restaurant-heavy town has subtle variations on salmon in leek sauce, and *berenjenas con miel* (fried aubergine with honey).
*Calle Nueva 10. Tel: 952 87 92 00.*

**Tragabuches** \*\*\*
Unbeaten the length and breadth of Andalucía, this Michelin-starred temple of *nueva cocida* goes from strength to strength and could be heading for a second Michelin star for its unique mix of local ingredients and traditional dishes mixed in outrageous new ways.
*José Aparicio 1. Tel: 952 19 02 91.*

## Sanlúcar de Barrameda
**Casa Bigote** **
*The* place to taste
*Sanluqueña* food: a
seafront bar and
restaurant in the
traditional Bajo de Guia
fishermen's *barrio*.
*Bajo de Guia. Tel: 953 26
26 96.*
**Mirador Doñana** **
This upmarket neighbour
to the Bigote has a less
funky take on Sanlúcar's
traditional fish and
seafood.
*Bajo de Guia. Tel: 956 36
42 05.*

## Seville
**La Albahaca** ***
This converted mansion
with movie-set interiors
has an excellent if
expensive traditional
menu.
*Plaza Santa Cruz 9.
Tel: 954 22 07 14.*
**Corral del Agua** **
Stylish courtyard
restaurant in an alley by
the Alcázar walls, with a
menu veering towards
*nueva cocida*.
*Callejón del Agua 6.
Tel: 954 5 22 07.*
**Egaña Oriza** **⁻***
One of the smartest
restaurants in town, with
a *nueva cocida* menu
(boar with pears and
prunes), on a corner of

the Alcázar gardens and
Plaza Don Juan de
Austria. The wonderful
*tapas* bar is highly
recommended.
*Calle San Fernando 41.
Tel: 954 22 72 54.*
**Enrique Becerra** **
Unassuming backstreet
*tapas* bar and restaurant
popular with locals and
the *New York Times* food
pages.
*Calle Gamazo 2. Tel: 954
21 30 49.*
**Hosteria El Laurel** **
Busy and popular
traditional restaurant
below the eponymous
hotel in a square in Santa
Cruz. Baked meats and
fish are a speciality, with
an excellent *friturada
variada* (batter-fried
seafood selection).
*Plaza de los Venerables 5.
Tel: 954 22 02 95.*
**El Kiosco de las Flores** *
A Triana institution, on
the river by the Triana
bridge, this is one of *the*
places to taste fish in
Seville.
*Calle del Betis s/n.*
**Taberna del
Alabardero** **
Another impressive
mansion conversion, with
a light international
menu.
*Calle Zaragoza 20.
Tel: 954 50 27 21.*

## Tarifa
**Arte Vida** *
Hotel-restaurant-gallery
just north of Tarifa, with
a beach restaurant
specialising in grilled fish,
meats, salad and pizzas.
*Carretera N340, 79.3km.
Tel: 956 68 52 46.*
**Casa Amarilla** *
Classic Andalucían
bodega specialising in
local ham, tuna and
cheese in the centre
of Tarifa's Sancho IV
party zone.
*Sancho IV El Bravo 9.
Tel: 956 68 19 93.*
**The Terrace** **
Probably the best
restaurant on the Tarifa
beach, set in the dense
subtropical gardens of the
trendy Hurricane Hotel.
*Hotel Hurricane, carretera
N340 78km. Tel: 956 68 49
19.*

## Úbeda **
**El Marqués**
This restaurant is in one
of Úbeda's two smartest
hotels, a 16th-century
mansion conversion.
The menu specialises in
traditional *Úbense* recipes
using local meat,
vegetables and fish from
the coast.
*Hotel Maria de Molino,
Plaza del Ayuntamiento.
Tel: 953 79 53 56.*

# Hotels and Accommodation

Andalucía is the most popular tourist destination in Spain and hotel numbers are increasing to meet that demand. Some industrial cities such as Huelva and Málaga are still poorly served with visitor accommodation, while some of the smallest pueblos now boast international quality boutique hotels.

Seville's plush Hotel Alfonso XIII

Below is a selection of mid-range to higher hotels across Andalucía which can be assumed to have en suite facilities, telephone, TV and, in a country where credit cards are not always accepted, take most credit cards.

**Booking**
Booking is advisable whenever possible, and an absolute must if you plan to visit during *Semana Santa*, the September ferias or any other local festivity.

Hotels will hold rooms until 6pm or later if you warn them of your estimated arrival time, but some may require pre-booking by credit card (and be warned that many do not quote prices inclusive of 17 per cent IVA, Spain's value added tax). Checkout is usually at noon, but most hotels will keep bags or even let you use the room until later if asked.

**Prices**
The prices shown according to the star system opposite are average summertime prices (although many Spanish hotels have year-round prices) for a double room. Suites and rooms during premium periods will be extra.

\*        under €50
\*\*      €50–100
\*\*\*    €100–150
\*\*\*\*  €150–250

**Almería**
**AM Torreluz** \*\*\*
This is one of the smartest hotels in the city. All mod cons, gym, sauna, spa and small rooftop terrace with pool. *Plaza Flores 5. Tel: 902 23 49 99. www.amhoteles.com.*
**Gran Hotel Almeria** \*\*\*
Large four-star convention-type hotel

Los Seises in Seville – a stunning renovation of a 16th-century palace

dating from the 1960s. Restaurant, bars, pool, but in a noisy part of town.
*Avenida Reina Regente 8. Tel: 950 23 80 11. www.granhotelalmeria.com.*

**Hotel La Perla** ★★
Almería's oldest hotel, recently refurbished, and a friendly budget option.
*Plaza del Carmen 7. Tel: 950 23 88 77.*

**Hotel Vincci Mediterráneo** ★★★
The trendiest hotel in Almería, with rooms and public spaces verging on *minimalista* style. Business facilities available.
*Avenida del Mediterráneo s/n. Tel: 950 62 42 72. www.vinccihotels.com.*

### Arcos de la Frontera
**Hotel El Convento** ★★
The best option in a town with few decent hotels. As the name suggests, this is a converted 17th-century convent on the edge of the precipice on which Arcos sits.
*Calle Maldonado 2. Tel: 956 70 23 33.*

**Hotel Marqués de Torresoto** ★★
More historic splendour in this renovated mansion with a patio overlooking the view.
*Calle Marqués de Torresoto 4. Tel: 956 70 07 17.*

### Arriate
**Arriadh Hotel** ★★
New five-room hotel, first in this town, with gardens, pool and great views.
*Estación Arriate s/n. Tel: 696 38 85 29.*

### Benaoján
**El Molino del Santo** ★★
Very pleasant English-owned country house hotel, with small bungalow-type rooms in mature gardens, an outdoor pool and lovely restaurant under willows by a tumbling mountain stream.
*Estación de Benaoján/Montejaque. Tel: 952 16 71 51. Closed: mid-Nov–mid-Feb.*

### Benarrabá
**Banu Rabbah** ★★
Launched as a collective by young people from this tiny *Pueblo Blanco*, this is the only hotel between Ronda and Gaucín. Twelve rooms, some with views over the mountains and all with spacious terraces.
*Calle Sierra Bermeja s/n. Tel: 952 15 02 88.*

### Bubión
**Las Terrazas** ★★
Spartan but comfortable and friendly family-run hotel with views to the south of this Alpujarran village.
*Plaza del Sol 7. Tel: 958 76 32 52.*

### Cádiz
**Francia y Paris** ★★
The best mid-range option in the old town, a central, quiet, if anonymous modern hotel behind a beautiful *belle époque* façade.
*Plaza de San Francisco 2. Tel: 956 22 23 48.*

**Playa Victoria** ★★★
Best of the beachside hotels in 'downtown' new Cádiz with stylish rooms and suites, all with sea views.
*Glorieta Ingeniero la Cierva 4. Tel: 956 27 54 11.*

### Carmona
**Alcázar de la Reina** ★★★
One of Carmona's fabulous 16th-

Mansion living in Ronda's 17th-century
San Gabriel

century mansions, sumptuously
renovated and sensitively modernised.
*Argollón s/n. Tel: 954 19 62 00.*
*www.alcazar-reina.es.*

**La Casa de Carmona ★★★★**
Gorgeous 16th-century palace
conversion in the beautiful town centre,
decorated with antiques and paintings.
*Plaza de Lasso 1. Tel: 954 14 33 00.*
*www.casadecarmon.com.*

### Cazorla
**Villa Turistica de Cazorla ★★**
Very pleasant hotel just on the edge of
this mountain town, a short walk from
the centre, with restaurant, gardens,
pools and views of the town.
*Ladera de San Isicio s/n. Tel: 953 71*
*01 00. www.villacazorla.com.*

### Conil de la Frontera
**Fuerte Conil ★★★**
Part of the Fuerte chain which has
hotels in Marbella and Grazalema, this is
the most comfortable of the Costa de la

Luz beach hotels, a large complex above
the beach with pools and restaurants.
Very popular with German and British
visitors.
*Playa de la Fontanilla. Tel: 956 44 33 44.*

### Córdoba
**Hotel Amistad Córdoba ★★★**
Tastefully modernised conversion of two
18th-century mansions on the edge of
La Juderia, the former Jewish *barrio*,
with a Mudéjar-style patio.
*Plaza de Maimonides 3. Tel: 957 42 03 35.*
**Hotel El Triunfo ★★**
Probably the best mid-price option here,
a friendly, traditional hotel on the
eastern side of the Mezquita, with bar
and restaurant and some rooms with
Mezquita views.
*Calle Corregidor Luis de la Cerda 79.*
*Tel: 957 47 55 00.*
**Hotel González ★★**
Former Moorish palace by the Mezquita,
with rooms looking onto a whitewashed
interior patio.
*Calle Manriquez 3. Tel: 957 47 98 19.*

### Cortes de la Frontera
**El Gecko ★★**
Cosy and friendly five-room hotel with
great restaurant (and pool) in idyllic
setting overlooking the river Guardiano.
*Estación de Cortes de la Frontera.*
*Tel: 952 15 33 15.*

### Gaucín
**Casablanca ★★**
Handsome mansion conversion with
exquisite gardens, pool and cod-Arabic
mirador.
*Teodoro Molino 12. Tel: 952 15 10 19.*
*Closed: Mon.*

**La Fructuosa** **
Five elegant modern suites with large terraces looking down towards the Rock and Africa.
*Calle Convento 67.*
*Tel: 952 15 10 72. www.lafructuosa.com.*

## Gibraltar
**Caleta** ***
Luxury hotel on the beach in this former fishing village at the other end of the Rock.
*Catalan Bay. Tel: 76501.*
*www.caletahotel.com.*
**Eliott Hotel** ***
The smartest central hotel, popular with business travellers.
*Governor's Parade. Tel: 70500.*
*www.gib.gi/eliotthotel.*
**The Rock** ***
The Gibraltarian institution, built by the Marquess of Bute in 1929 and totally refurbished in 2000. All rooms sea-facing, restaurants, bars and a pool.
*Europa Road. Tel: 73000.*
*www.rockhotelgibraltar.com.*

## Granada
**Hotel America** **
This is the ideal place to stay in Granada, a lovely old mansion deep inside the Alhambra. Booking ahead advised.
*Real de al Alhambra 53.*
*Tel: 958 22 74 70. www.hamerica.com.*
**Hotel Carmen de Santa Inés** **
Like its sister hotel the Palacio de Santa Inés, this is an exquisitely refurbished mansion, with suites off a column-lined courtyard with fountain.
*Placeta Porras 7.*
*Tel: 958 22 63 80.*

**Hotel Juan Miguel** **
Central hotel, near the Puerta Real, and a decent mid-range option.
*Acero del Darro 24. Tel: 958 52 11 11.*
**Hotel Macia**
Pleasantly modernised townhouse hotel on this central square.
*Plaza Nueva 4. Tel: 958 22 75 36.*
**Hotel Triunfo** ***
Smart, modern hotel at the far end of Gran Via, quieter than some of the more central hotels.
*Plaza del Triunfo 19. Tel: 958 20 74 44.*
**Palacio de Santa Inés** ***
Renovated 16th-century mansion in the heart of Granada's Moorish Albaicín *barrio*, with just seven rooms around a beautiful courtyard.
*Cuesta de Santa Inés 9.*
*Tel: 958 22 23 62.*
**Reina Cristina** **
Handy central mid-price hotel in a fairly quiet side street. Another restored mansion, this is famous for being the last abode of the poet Lorca (*see p24*), who was arrested here and executed after the fall of the republic. (Lorca's room was where room no 310 is now.)
*Tablas 4. Tel: 958 25 32 11.*
*www.hotelreinacristina.com.*

## Grazalema
**Hostal Casa de las Piedras** *
Excellent if modest hotel, with a fine restaurant and a friendly atmosphere.
*Calle las Piedras 32. Tel: 956 13 20 14.*
**Puerta de la Villa** ***
This is a stylishly renovated mansion hotel with spectacular views, restaurant, sauna and gym.
*Plaza Pequeña 8.*
*Tel: 956 13 23 76.*

## Guadix

### Hotel Pedro Antonio Alarcón ✶✶

Guadix is close enough to Granada or Almería to make it a day's round trip, but if you want to share the cave-life experience, this unique hotel offers cave suites, gardens and pool.

*Barriada san Torcuan. Tel: 958 66 49 86. www.andalucia.com/cavehotel.*

## Jaén

### Condestable Iranzo ✶✶

Central, modern and comfortable hotel in the town centre.

*Paseo de la Estación 32. Tel: 953 22 28 00.*

### Hotel Europa ✶✶

Another central hotel, recently renovated with modernist décor.

*Plaza de Belén 1. Tel: 953 22 27 00.*

## Jerez

### Avenida Jerez

Large, modern, convention-type hotel on one of Jerez's major boulevards, a short walk from the centre.

*Avenida Alcalde Domecq 10. Tel: 956 34 74 11.*

### Doña Blanca ✶✶

Probably the best mid-range option in Jerez, a pleasant modern hotel in a backstreet just yards from Jerez's busy central market.

*Calle Bodéga 11. Tel: 956 34 87 16.*

## Jimena

### Hostal El Anón ✶

Hotel-restaurant, built around a warren of tiny courtyards, with a rooftop pool.

*Calle Consuelo 34–40. Tel: 956 64 01 13.*

## Málaga

### Don Curro ✶✶

This is one of the best hotels in Málaga: simple, modern and comfortable, set back from the busy Alameda.

*Calle Sancha de Lara 7 . Tel: 952 22 72 00.*

### Hotel Las Vegas ✶✶

Another decent Alameda-area option,

Tarifa's Hurricane gardens, with pool and sea beyond

close to the beach; modern and purpose built, with its own pool.
*Paseo de Sancha 22. Tel: 952 21 77 12.*

## Marbella
### El Faro *
The best budget option in town: a simple, friendly, purpose-built apart-hotel on a quiet street between the beach and the main street.
*Calle Virgen del Pilar 11.*
*Tel: 952 77 42 30.*
### Hotel Fuerte ***
On its own avenida, rooms have partial or full sea views, two pools, gym and spa, beach club.
*Avenida el Fuerte. Tel: 952 86 15 00.*
*www.hotel.elfuerte.es.*
### Marbella Inn **
Slightly more comfortable than the Faro, with restaurant and rooftop pool.
*Calle Jacinto Benavente s/n.*
*Tel: 952 82 54 87.*
### La Morada Mas Hermosa **
Best mid-range hotel in Marbella, prettily renovated in the old town with just five individually decorated suites around a tiny courtyard.
*Calle Montenebros 16a.*
*Tel: 952 92 44 67.*

## Ronda
### Acinipo **
This mixes avant-garde design with classic Spanish décor, and is ideally situated away from traffic and with excellent mountain views.
*Calle José Aparacio 7. Tel: 952 16 10 02.*
*www.hotelacinipo.com.*
### Alavera de los Baños **
Ronda's most charming hotel: a row of 19th-century tanners' cottages converted

Concealed inside a country *cortijo*, El Juncal mixes Manhattan-style minimalism with a warm Andalucían welcome

into a Hispano-Arabic styled hotel with a terrace restaurant and pool.
*Calle San Miguel s/n. Tel: 952 87 91 43.*
### La Casona de la Ciudad **
Impressively grand town mansion conversion in the old town.
*Calle Marqués de Salvatierra 5.*
*Tel: 952 87 95 95.*
### La Cazalla **
A short drive or cab ride out of Ronda, on a Roman road in its own secret valley, this incomparable little hotel has just six suites, all individually designed. Great food, wild gardens and a 12th-century plunge pool.
*El Tajo Abanico, 4km (2.4 miles) from Ronda. Tel: 952 11 41 75.*
*www.andalucia.com/accommodation/laca zalla.*

**Fuente de la Higuera** **
This sumptuously renovated country
house outside Ronda is run more as a
help-yourself house party.
*Partido de Frontones. Tel: 952 11 43 95.*

**El Juncal** **
Cool, minimalist designer hotel, a
former *cortijo* (farmhouse) transformed
with great style under the aegis of
Tragabuches. Sauna and a wild, sloped
walk-in pool.
*Carretera Ronda–El Burgo.*
*Tel: 952 16 11 70. www.eljuncal*

**San Gabriel** **
This 18th-century mansion was the first
hotel in Ronda's *casco antiguo*, renovated
with great care by the Peréz family, who
are gracious hosts.
*Calle José María Holgado 19.*
*Tel: 952 19 03 92.*

**Sanlúcar de Barrameda**

**Posada de Palacio** *
A short walk from the town centre, this
is a former manzanilla bodega, built
around a central courtyard.
*Calle Caballeros 11. Tel: 956 36 48 40.*

**Tartaneros** **
A grand mansion from Sanlúcar's
wealthier days, in a central town square,
decorated with antiques.
*Tartaneros 8. Tel: 956 36 20 44.*

**Seville**

**Casa Numero 7** ***
This small, intimate hotel is actually a
private home, lovingly decorated with
artefacts from the family art collection.
*Calle Virgenes 7. Tel: 954 22 15 81.*

**Las Casas de la Juderia** ***
Exquisitely refurbished mansion, in
parts dating back to the 16th century.

*Plaza de Santa Maria la Blanca, callejón
de Dos Hermanas 7. Tel: 954 41 51 50.*

**Las Casas de los Mercaderes** ***
One of the best situated hotels in this
noisy city, on a pedestrian street a short
walk from the cathedral.
*Calle Alvarez Quintero 9–13.*
*Tel: 954 22 68 58.*

**Doña Maria** **
Handsomely remodelled townhouse.
*Don Remondo 19. Tel: 954 22 49 90.*

**Hosteria del Laurel** **
A bargain in the heart of Santa Cruz,
above the popular restaurant on the
ground floor.
*Plaza de los Venerables 9. Tel: 954 21 51 07.*

**Hotel Simon** **
Friendly and popular mid-price option.
Another 18th-century mansion
conversion, this is often busy all year
round.
*Garcia Vinuesa 19. Tel: 954 22 66 60.*

**San Gil** ***
Away from the centre, this is a pleasant
renovation of a 1901 townhouse with a
courtyard, gardens and pool.
*Calle Parras 28. Tel: 954 90 68 11.*

**Los Seises** ****
A stunning renovation of a 16th-century
palace in the shadow of the Giralda.
*Calle Segovias 6. Tel: 954 22 94 95.*

**Tarifa**

**Casa Amarilla** **
Stylish early 19th-century apartment
hotel, with each suite individually
designed.
*Sancho IV El Bravo 9. Tel: 956 68 19 93.*

**Arte Vida** **
Funky beach hotel, gallery and
restaurant, just north of town.
*Carretera N340 78km. Tel: 956 68 52 46.*

**Hotel Hurricane** \*\*\*
Notoriously difficult to book into, but
with comfortable if simple rooms,
beautiful gardens and pool.
*Carretera N340 78km.*
*Tel: 956 68 49 19.*

## Úbeda
**María de Molina** \*\*
Beautifully renovated 16th-century
mansion with enclosed patio and
incredible views.
*Plaza del Ayuntamiento s/n. Tel: 953 79
53 56. www.hotel-de-molina.com.*
**Palacio de Rambla** \*\*
Authentic 16th-century *palacio* on the
edge of Úbeda's old town.
*Plaza del Marquéz 1.*
*Tel: 953 75 01 96.*

## Vejer de la Frontera
**La Casa del Califa** \*\*
The folks from Tarifa's Hurricane have
restyled this beautiful old property into
an elegant boutique hotel.
*Plaza de España 16.*
*Tel: 956 44 77 30.*
*www.vejer.com.*
**Hotel Convento San Francisco** \*
Converted convent at the heart of this
gorgeous *Pueblo Blanco.*
*La Plazuela. Tel: 956 45 10 02/3/4.*

## Zahara de la Sierra
**Hostal Marqués de la Sierra** \*
Friendly family-run mansion conversion
is the best-kept secret among the *Pueblos
Blancos.*
*Calle San Juan 3. Tel: 956 12 30 61.*

De-stress in style at Fuente de la Higuera

# Practical Guide

## Arriving and Getting Around
### Entry Formalities

Visitors from EU countries, Iceland and Norway can enter Spain with a valid national identity card, although visitors from countries without ID cards such as Britain need a valid passport. Citizens of Canada, New Zealand and the USA do not need visas if they are staying for no more than 90 days. Visitors from Australia will need a visa if intending to stay longer than 30 days. It is always advisable to confirm current visa regulations, either with a tour company, airline or consulate, before travelling.

In theory, anyone planning to stay in Spain for more than 90 days should report to the police to register their presence. In reality, nobody does, and the police would be bemused and not a

You will find tourist information at every airport and major rail station

little irritated if you tried. The situation changes if you intend to live and work in Spain, which will involve registering your residency and negotiating the Spanish employment, tax and welfare systems. However, the government is currently planning to simplify matters for EU citizens travelling and working in Spain. People visiting purely for leisure purposes should have no fear of Spanish bureaucracy.

### By Air

Andalucía has five major international airports – Almería, Granada, Jerez de la Frontera, Málaga and Seville – plus the 'offshore' option of flights into Gibraltar. Málaga is by far the easiest international option, with flights from around Europe, north Africa and north American hub airports, as well as international connections via Madrid. Both Seville and Granada have regular international services, and Almería, is expanding its network of air connections. Spain's national airline **Iberia** (*tel: 902 400 500*) operates national and international routes out of them all.

Seville's **San Pablo** airport (*tel: 954 44 99 00*) is 12km (7.4 miles) northeast of the city and a simple journey by car, taxi or bus (*half-hourly, 6.30am–11.30pm*) to the centre. Buses stop at the vast **Santa Justa** railway station, which has connections to all Andalucían cities and most towns (see below).

Málaga's **Pablo Ruiz Picasso** airport (*tel: 952 24 88 04*) is 6km (3.7 miles) west of the city and the most easily accessible of all Andalucían airports. As well as taxis and buses (*half-hourly, 6.30am–11.30pm*) there is also a handy suburban train connection just a few minutes' walk from the airport and signed from the arrivals and departures halls. This line, the Málaga–Fuengirola line, has a half-hourly service in both directions (*7am–11.30pm, 15mins, daily; pay on board*). Anyone wanting to travel onwards by bus or train should get off at Estación RENFE, one stop before the terminus at Centro/Alameda, as advised by the automatic announcements on the train. The Málaga–Fuengirola station is below the main RENFE station here, and both are a short walk away from the Estación de Autobuses.

**By Car**
Visiting Seville and Andalucía from abroad by car is more an adventure than

Always leave plenty of time to negotiate ticket office queues

a comfortable option, but it is possible. Seville is roughly 600km (372 miles) from Spain's northern and southern borders with France, and a day's drive from either Barcelona or Bilbao, which has handy ferry links to Britain and northern mainland Europe.

**Driving**
The best map (*see p.187, Maps*) to negotiate Andalucía by any form of transport is the Michelin 446 España: Andalucía/Costa del Sol 1/400,000. Many first-time visitors to Andalucía are surprised at how mountainous much of it is, and although many of the roads are excellent this fact should be borne in mind when hiring and driving cars here. Similarly, a special warning has to be issued about the N340, the *autovia* (motorway) that skirts Andalucía's coastline. It is said to be the most dangerous motorway in Europe.

The Spanish drive on the right, along with most continental Europeans. The quality of driving in Spain is as bad as in most Mediterranean countries, and particularly so in cities. Traffic offences can lead to on-the-spot fines and the police may even accompany you to an ATM. Seatbelt use is obligatory. Speed limits are 120kph on autovias, 100kph on other roads and just 50kph in built up areas. *Bandas de sonoras* (speed bumps) are common in dormitory areas. Drink-driving is forbidden. Check cover for accident, theft of vehicle and liability with your travel insurer.

Petrol (*gasolina*) is available from *gasolineras* (petrol stations) as *super*, *normal* (both leaded), *sin plomo* (unleaded) and *gasoil* (diesel).

*Gasolineras* are plentiful in and on the outskirts of cities and towns, but grow scarce in the countryside.

**Car Hire**
You will need to produce your passport and an EU or international driving licence to rent a car in Spain. The law requires that all cars carry a red warning triangle and replacement headlight bulbs – ask the rental company to confirm that these comply with regulations, as the police have been known to crack down on certain types of warning triangle, for example.

International companies such as **Avis** (*tel: 902 13 55 31; www.avis.es*), **Budget** (*tel: 901 20 12 12*), **Europcar** (*tel: 901 10 20 20; www.europcar.com*) and **Hertz** (*tel: 902 402 405; www.hertz.es*) have offices at all airports and in most city and town centres.

Fly-drive deals are often worth investigating, although hire cars with the company's livery are sometimes targeted by snatch burglars. Enquire about cars without livery, or whether it can be removed during your hire.

**By Coach**
Coach (*autobus*) is the most popular and cheapest form of transport in Spain. Services are more frequent than trains and reach more destinations. The downside is that of most coach travel: apart from sleek inter-city and international services, local coach stock is basic, sometimes aged, and while the standard of driving is excellent the experience can leave much to be desired.

*Estaciónes de autobuses* are commonly found (and signed) on the perimeter of the city centre, such as Seville's Prado de San Sebastian (*tel: 954 41 71 11*) for southbound buses, and Plaza des Armas (*tel: 954 22 26 93*) for westbound services. The bus system is privatised, with as many as six or more different companies operating different routes, and they vary from city to city and town to town.

Pre-booking is possible only at bus stations and it is common to pay on board for all but long-distance routes. If you are travelling only part of the bus's route – Seville to Jerez, say, when it continues on to Cádiz – don't be surprised if you are told to wait until a few minutes before departure before being allowed to purchase a ticket, as long-distance passengers often get preferential service. If it looks as though a bus is filling up, some canny travellers just say they're going to the final stop and pay the extra fare. Be warned that bus services around weekends are often pre-booked by students returning home and families on the move.

**By Train**
With sufficient time on your hands, trains are the most comfortable and scenic way to explore Andalucía. It is even possible to visit from northern Europe, although an average journey from London or Paris would take two days. The price, more than the cost of a first-class air ticket, may well deter all but fanatical train buffs.

Seville's **Santa Justa** station (*tel: 902 24 02 02*) sits at the centre of Andalucía's rail network. It's advisable to book ahead for any journeys between cities, particularly in summertime. Many

Autobuses connect almost every city and village

services pass through the central junction of Bobadilla, and it is possible that one section of your journey, Bobadilla to Granada or Seville, may be fully booked if you try to buy tickets on the day.

If pre-booking is not possible, leave plenty of time to purchase a ticket using the lengthy queuing system in all major stations. Anyone planning to travel around Andalucía should also check services and availability before making any firm plans involving train travel. Spain's RENFE (Red Nacíonal de Ferrocarilles Españoles) train system is modernising numerous lines, which will provide better services but will also involve years of engineering works which may affect your journey. RENFE has a website (*www.renfe.es*) with information in Spanish and English, and a phone line (*tel: 902 24 02 02*). The phone line is Spanish, but there are operators fluent in English and other languages. Alternatively, ask a hotel for assistance, or try one of Spain's two

major travel agencies, Halcon Viajes and Viajes Marsans, who have offices in all cities and towns and deal with domestic rail and coach travel as well as holidays abroad.

### Children

Children under four travel free on public transport. Hotels operate various systems: young children often stay free, and older children at reduced rates, while family rooms with three or more beds are common in most hotels. Entry to state-owned museums is often free to under-18s, although some charge youth/student rates. There are sometimes reductions for under-12s, and special student rates for certain galleries, museums and concert halls.

### Climate

It is impossible to make any generalisations about the climate in Andalucía, except perhaps to hazard that east of Málaga tends to be driest in winter. Anything west of Ronda is prone to whatever is brewing out in the Atlantic. The early 21st century has seen the world entering another *el niño* event, when inversions in temperature in the southern Pacific affect global weather trends. It is possible to sunbathe on January 1, but it is just as possible to experience snow on January 2. Most commonly, Andalucía remains dry between May and September, with temperatures in the 20–30°C (70–90°F) range. Apart from the interior of Almería province and *el sartén* (the frying pan), around Écija east of Seville, temperatures rarely rise above 100°F, and this is usually a dry heat. Autumn

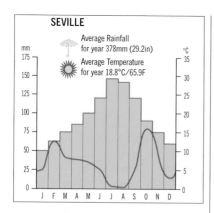

**SEVILLE**

Average Rainfall for year 378mm (29.2in)

Average Temperature for year 18.8°C/65.9F

**Weather Conversion Chart**
25.4mm = 1 inch
°F = 1.8 x °C + 32

| | Conversion Table | |
|---|---|---|
| FROM | TO | MULTIPLY BY |
| Inches | Centimetres | 2.54 |
| Feet | Metres | 0.3048 |
| Yards | Metres | 0.9144 |
| Miles | Kilometres | 1.6090 |
| Acres | Hectares | 0.4047 |
| Gallons | Litres | 4.5460 |
| Ounces | Grams | 28.35 |
| Pounds | Grams | 453.6 |
| Pounds | Kilograms | 0.4536 |
| Tons | Tonnes | 1.0160 |

To convert back, for example from centimetres to inches, divide by the number in the third column.

weather becomes unpredictable around late October, and the best advice to travellers packing with weather in mind is to take layers and a waterproof. If you are travelling from the coast into the interior and/or mountains, expect a temperature drop of 10°F or more.

### Crime

Crime is less prevalent in Seville and Andalucía than in northern Europe, but the proximity of a tourism culture to serious unemployment and poverty can create problems. Most crimes are opportunistic, and Seville and Granada are known for the frequency of car break-ins and random bag snatches. However, commonsense behaviour with vehicles, valuables and personal safety should protect the visitor against all but the most unfortunate incidents. Park in secured pay parking or hotel car parks where possible, and remove all your valuables whenever and wherever you

**Men's Suits**

| UK | | 36 | 38 | 40 | 42 | 44 | 46 | 48 |
|---|---|---|---|---|---|---|---|---|
| Rest of Europe | 46 | 48 | 50 | 52 | 54 | 56 | 58 |
| US | | 36 | 38 | 40 | 42 | 44 | 46 | 48 |

**Dress Sizes**

| UK | | 8 | 10 | 12 | 14 | 16 | 18 |
|---|---|---|---|---|---|---|---|
| France | | 36 | 38 | 40 | 42 | 44 | 46 |
| Italy | | 38 | 40 | 42 | 44 | 46 | 48 |
| Rest of Europe | 34 | 36 | 38 | 40 | 42 | 44 |
| US | | 6 | 8 | 10 | 12 | 14 | 16 |

**Men's Shirts**

| UK | 14 | 14.5 | 15 | 15.5 | 16 | 16.5 | 17 |
|---|---|---|---|---|---|---|---|
| Rest of Europe | 36 | 37 | 38 | 39/40 | 41 | 42 | 43 |
| US | 14 | 14.5 | 15 | 15.5 | 16 | 16.5 | 17 |

**Men's Shoes**

| UK | | 7 | 7.5 | 8.5 | | 9.5 | 10.5 | 11 |
|---|---|---|---|---|---|---|---|---|
| Rest of Europe | 41 | 42 | 43 | | 44 | 45 | 46 |
| US | | 8 | 8.5 | 9.5 | 10.5 | 11.5 | 12 |

**Women's Shoes**

| UK | | 4.5 | 5 | 5.5 | | 6 | 6.5 | 7 |
|---|---|---|---|---|---|---|---|---|
| Rest of Europe | 38 | 38 | 39 | 39 | 40 | 41 |
| US | | 6 | 6.5 | 7 | 7.5 | 8 | 8.5 |

park overnight. Don't carry expensive valuables around with you, and take care of obvious targets such as cameras and bags.

It is important, however, to maintain a sense of perspective: you are no more likely to be robbed or attacked here than anywhere else in Europe, and certainly less than in any large north American city. Serious crimes are rare. If you are the victim of a crime, report it to the police as soon as possible, and enlist the assistance of hotels and others if possible.

### Customs Regulations

The duty-free allowance for visitors to Spain is: 800 cigarettes or 200 cigars, 10 litres of spirits and 90 litres of wine, 20 litres of fortified wine, 110 litres of beer, 60 centilitres of perfume and 250 centilitres of toilet water. There is no limit on the amount of money you may bring into Spain, although if you bring in large sums of cash, some way beyond expected living costs and likely purchases, you may be required by customs to prove that it is legal tender.

### Documents and Insurance

Tourists need to carry their passport or national identity card with them at all times. Drivers should always ensure that they have their papers with them, as this is how most visitors may find themselves encountering the police.

### Embassies and Consulates

Almost every country has an embassy or consulate in Spain, although usually in Madrid. Some, such as Britain, also have consulates in Fuengirola, Málaga and Seville. Depending on your particular enquiry, it may be best to try Madrid before contacting a local office.

### Madrid

**Australia** *Plaza del Descubridor, Diego Ordás 3. Tel: 914 42 53 62.*
**Canada** *Nuñez de Balboa 35. Tel: 914 31 43 00.*
**UK** *Fernando el Santo 16. Tel: 913 19 02 00.*
**USA** *Serrano 75. Tel: 915 77 40 00.*

### Fuengirola, Málaga and Seville

**Australia** *calle Federico Rubio 14, Seville. Tel: 954 22 09 71.*
**Canada** *Edificio Horizonte, Plaza Malagueta 3, Málaga. Tel: 952 22 33 46.*
**Ireland** *Galerias Santa Monica, Avenida Boliches 15, Fuengirola. Tel: 952 47 51 08.*
**Netherlands** *Alameda de Colon, Málaga. Tel: 952 70 07 20.*
**UK** *Plaza Nueva 8, Seville. Tel: 954 22 88 75 (also Málaga: tel: 952 21 75 71).*
**US** *Paseo de las Delicias 7, Seville. Tel: 954 23 18 85.*

### Emergency Telephone Numbers

**Ambulance** (*ambulancia*) 112
**Fire brigade** (*bomberos*) 080
**General emergencies** (*urgencias*) 092
**Local police** 092
**Medical emergencies** (*doctor*) 061

### Health and Insurance

EU citizens are entitled to free emergency treatment in Spain, but some non-urgent treatments are only available privately, which is why it is important for all visitors to Spain to arrange private travel insurance to cover treatment and the costs of repatriation.

## LANGUAGE

Many people working in hotels and restaurants will want to practise their English on you, but any attempt to speak Spanish will win you friends among the Spanish. Although in some respects it is a more complicated language than English, in one respect it is easier: words are pronounced as they look, according to a few simple rules.

### PRONUNCIATION

Generally the accent falls on the second-to-last syllable unless it is marked with a written accent.

### Vowel Sounds

Vowels are always pronounced in the same way:

| | | | |
|---|---|---|---|
| a | ah | o | oh |
| e | eh | u | oo |
| i | ee | | |

### Consonant Sounds

Consonants are the same as in English with the following exceptions:

| | |
|---|---|
| ll | like 'y' in 'yes' |
| rr | is rolled, as in Scotland |
| h | is silent |
| j | like a guttural 'h' |
| g | followed by 'e' or 'i' like a guttural 'h' |
| ñ | Like 'nio' as in 'onion' |

### USEFUL WORDS AND PHRASES

| | |
|---|---|
| yes | si |
| no | no |
| please | por favor |
| thank you | gracias |
| you are welcome | de nada |
| bon appetit | buen provecho |
| hello | hola |
| goodbye | adiós |
| morning | mañana |
| good morning | buenos días |
| afternoon/evening | tarde |
| good afternoon/ good evening | buenas tardes |
| night | noche |
| good night | buenas noches |
| cheap | barato |
| expensive | caro |
| near | cerca |
| far | lejos |
| day | dia |
| week | semana |
| month | mes |
| year | año |

### NUMBERS

| | |
|---|---|
| 1 | uno |
| 2 | dos |
| 3 | tres |
| 4 | cuatro |
| 5 | cinco |
| 6 | seis |
| 7 | siete |
| 8 | ocho |
| 9 | nueve |
| 10 | diez |

### DAYS OF THE WEEK

| | |
|---|---|
| Sunday | domingo |
| Monday | lunes |
| Tuesday | martes |
| Wednesday | miércoles |
| Thursday | jueves |
| Friday | viernes |
| Saturday | sábado |

For British visitors, an E111 form will cover most eventualities, but some treatments may require payment which can be claimed back later. Non-urgent cases can be dealt with at a local Centro de Salud during surgery hours.

There are no vaccine requirements to enter Spain.

## Chemists

There is always one *farmacia* (chemist) open 24 hours a day in any district of a city and in most large towns, identified by a flashing green cross above the entrance. *Farmacias* usually display a list of who is open when in their windows. Chemists are allowed to diagnose minor ailments and prescribe certain over-the-counter drugs to treat these. Not all over-the-counter drugs (antihistamines, for example) are as freely available in Spain as elsewhere.

## Maps

There are numerous maps of Andalucía and its cities and regions, including the aforementioned Michelin 446. The best map shop in Andalucía is in the centre of Seville: **LTC** (*Avenida Menéndez Pelayo 42; tel: 954 42 59 64; email: ltc-mapas@sp-editores.es*), just beyond the Jardines de Murillo behind the Alcázar. In Britain, **Stanfords** of London (*12–14 Long Acre, WC2; tel: 020 7836 1321; www.stanfords.co.uk*) is opening stores around Britain. In Australia, try **Mapland** (*tel: 03 96 70 43 83; www.mapland.com.au*) in Melbourne; and in the United States **Traveler's Choice** (*22 W 52nd St, NY; tel: 212 941 1535; email: tvlchoice@aol.co*m).

For further tourist and map information try the Spanish tourism authorities at *www.tourspain.org* and for Andalucía *www.andalucia.org*.

Each town and village has a *centro de salud*, health centre, that can help with emergencies

## Media

Most international editions of British, continental European and US newspapers such as the *Wall Street Journal* and *Herald Tribune* are available on the day of publication in Seville and other larger cities and towns. Few hotels have any international satellite television channels apart from CNN and some dedicated French and German cable/satellite channels.

## National Holidays

**1 January** Año Nuevo (New Year's Day)
**6 January** Día de los Reyes (Epiphany)
**28 February** Día de Andalucía (regional holiday)
**19 March** San José (St Joseph's Day)

**March or April** (variable) Viernes Santo (Good Friday)
**1 May** Día del Trabajo (Labour Day)
**15 May** San Isidro (St Isidore's Day)
**May or June** (variable) Corpus Christi
**15 August** Asunción de la Virgen (Assumption of the Blessed Virgin Mary)
**12 October** Día de la Hispanidad (National Day of Spain)
**1 November** Todos los Santos (All Saints' Day)
**6 December** Día de la Constitución (Constitution Day)
**8 December** Inmaculada Concepción (Immaculate Conception)
**25 December** Día de Navidad (Christmas Day)

Cities and most large towns will have at least one *libreria*, paper shop, stocking international publications

## Time
Spain follows Central European Time, which is GMT (Greenwich Mean Time) plus one hour, or US EST (Eastern Standard Time) plus six hours.

## Toilets
Public toilets are a rarity in Andalucía, as in the rest of Spain, although most department stores and public monuments have them. A café or bar is the best alternative, although more and more bars are posting *solo clientes* (clients only) signs on the doors to their *aseos* (toilets), so a soft drink is often your ticket for entry.

## Tourist Information
There are tourist information desks, clearly signed by a large letter *i*, in every airport, and in the centre of every city and town. Some, such as Seville and Granada, have more than one. The central office in Seville is on Avenida de la Constitución (*tel: 954 22 14 04*).

There are cashpoint machines in most towns

## ACKNOWLEDGEMENTS

Thomas Cook Publishing wishes to thank the photographers, picture libraries and other organisations for the loan of the photographs reproduced in this book, to whom the copyright in the photographs belong.

PATRONATO DE TURISMO DE LA COSTA DEL SOL for photographs reproduced on pages 97, 159, 161, 165, 172 and 177.

The remaining pictures were supplied by MICHELLE CHAPLOW/ANDALUCÍA SLIDE LIBRARY.

**Copy-editing:** Katy Carter

**Index:** Indexing Specialists (UK) Ltd

**Maps:** IFA Design Ltd, Plymouth, UK

**Proof-reading:** Cambridge Publishing Management Ltd and Richard Hall